CHARITABLE
GIVING
AND
GOVERNMENT
POLICY

Recent Titles in
Contributions in Economics and Economic History

CHARITABLE GIVING AND GOVERNMENT POLICY

An Economic Analysis

JERALD SCHIFF

CONTRIBUTIONS IN ECONOMICS
AND ECONOMIC HISTORY,
NUMBER 102

GREENWOOD PRESS
New York · Westport, Connecticut · London

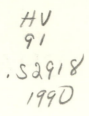

HV
91
.S2918
1990

Library of Congress Cataloging-in-Publication Data

Schiff, Jerald Alan.
   Charitable giving and government policy : an economic analysis /
Jerald Schiff.
     p. cm.—(Contributions in economics and economic history,
ISSN 0084-9235 ; no. 102)
     Includes bibliographical references.
     ISBN 0-313-25747-7 (lib. bdg. : alk. paper)
     1. Charities—United States—Finance. 2. United States—Social
policy—1980- 3. Voluntarism—United States. I. Title.
II. Series.
HV91.S2918 1990
361.7'0970—dc20   89-37978

British Library Cataloguing in Publication Data is available.

Library of Congress Catalog Card Number: 89-37978
ISBN: 0-313-25747-7
ISSN: 0084-9235

First published in 1990

Greenwood Press, Inc.
88 Post Road West, Westport, Connecticut 06881

Printed in the United States of America

The paper used in this book complies with the
Permanent Paper Standard issued by the National
Information Standards Organization (Z39.48–1984).

10 9 8 7 6 5 4 3 2 1

Contents

Tables and Figures

CHARITABLE
GIVING
AND
GOVERNMENT
POLICY

1.

Giving and Government: An Introduction

The 1980s have seen several policy changes that directly affect the behavior and health of the charitable sector of the economy. Perhaps the two most obvious changes are, first, the sharp reduction in the rate of growth of government social welfare spending and, second, the Tax Reform Act of 1986.

As government's role as a provider of social services has been reduced, increased emphasis has been placed on private, voluntary provision of these services, financed by charitable contributions. A lively debate has ensued over the extent to which charitable organizations can compensate for government cutbacks. At the same time as charities have been asked to "fill the gap," however, government support for the charitable sector—in the form of grants and purchases of service—has fallen as well,[1] so that charities find themselves pinched between raised expectations and fewer resources.

The Tax Reform Act of 1986 has, in addition, reduced the incentives for many individuals to give to charity. By sharply reducing the number of itemizers, lowering tax rates, and eliminating the tax deductibility of donations for non-itemizers, tax reform has raised the price of a money donation for the typical donor, thus discouraging charitable giving.

The impact of these changes on the charitable sector is of great interest to policy makers, nonprofit organization leaders, and donors alike. In this book, I provide a framework for analyzing the impact of these, and other, policies on charitable giving of money and time. The analysis is "economic" in the sense that decisions regarding charitable giving are assumed to be made in a rational manner and are viewed as conceptually similar to other consumption decisions.

Decisions regarding giving are, however, unusual in several important ways. First, the output financed by a charitable gift is generally collective, in the sense that it simultaneously benefits, or enters the utility function of, many individuals. So, for instance, if I "buy" an hour of public television by making a charitable gift, all viewers benefit. In a similar fashion, if I finance a shipment of food to the needy, not only is the needy recipient made better off, but so am I and so, in fact, are all those who value increased food consumption by the needy.

Economists are typically pessimistic regarding the ability of voluntary action to provide collective goods. Individuals desiring such goods, it is argued, will attempt to "free ride" on the contributions of others, with the end result that collective goods are not provided, or at least provided in less than optimal quantities.[2] Thus, government—with its power to coerce payment via the tax system—is largely relied upon to provide goods of a collective nature. While the existence of a charitable sector that relies heavily on donations for its existence makes it clear that this analysis oversimplifies, the collective nature of much charitable output does have important implications for an economic analysis of charitable giving.

First, because governments provide goods and services that may be viewed by donors as similar to the output of charities, donor behavior may be influenced by government spending decisions. If, for instance, government provision of social services to the poor is viewed by a consumer as generous, he or she may have little demand for additional services provided by private charities and, so, may not give much to charity.

By the same token, giving by any one individual will be influenced by the behavior of other donors. I may value redistribution to the needy, for instance, but would prefer that such redistribution came out of your pocket (assuming you are not one of the needy) than mine. If you, then, increase your giving, I may reduce mine and free ride. Thus, any economic analysis of charitable behavior should account for interactions both between government and individual donors as well as among donors.

Giving decisions are also unusual—although hardly unique—in that donors often have poor information about the marginal impact of their gift. That is, they may be far from certain just what their donation is buying. If I send a dollar to CARE, it is prohibitively costly for me to determine how that dollar is used. This "asymmetric information"—the charity has more information than the donor about the use of a gift—has a number of implications for the analysis.

First, it helps explain why organizations that rely on donations for revenue virtually always take the form of nonprofit organizations, as opposed to ordinary for-profit firms. Hansmann (1980) argued that the legal constraint facing nonprofit firms—namely, that no surplus earned by the firm can be distributed to its owners—reduces the incentive of nonprofits to cheat poorly informed donors.

Second—and more central to the issues raised in this book—asymmetric information provides additional avenues for government policies to influence charitable giving. Increased support by government of a charitable organization may provide information to potential donors about the quality of that organization, thereby encouraging private giving. Conversely, the recent reductions in government support for many nonprofit organizations may make donors less willing to trust nonprofits to make good use of their gifts.[3]

Finally, the donor's lack of information may explain, at least in part, why much voluntary support of charities comes, not in the form of money, but rather as donated time, or volunteer labor. Donors may believe that by volunteering they are better able to monitor the use made of their gift than if they donate cash.

Volunteering, and its relationship to government policies, is considered in detail in this book. This research seeks to fill a gap in the economic analysis of charitable behavior. Previous work in this area has largely ignored volunteering, focusing on contributions of money.[4] This is a rather large gap, since volunteering is of approximately equal value to the charitable sector as money donations. In 1984, hours donated by volunteers to nonprofit organizations were valued at $80 billion. This compares with the $73.3 billion of money contributions in the same year.[5]

A key question addressed in this book is why individuals would give time, in particular, rather than money. A number of potential motives for volunteering are considered, in addition to the "information" motive noted above. For instance, volunteering is viewed as a means of acquiring influence over the activities of a charity, or as a way to develop job skills that will increase future earnings for the volunteer. Each of the various models of volunteering has implications for the impact of government tax, spending, and regulatory policies on giving of time and of money.

The analysis of charitable giving presented here generates a number of testable hypotheses. Using survey and other data, I provide evidence on the relevance of the various models and estimate the effects of changes in government policies on giving of money and time. The picture that emerges is one in which money and time donations play very different roles and in which government policies can have a significant impact on giving and, so, the health of the charitable sector.

The Bush administration has pointed to a continued, and perhaps increased, reliance on the charitable sector with its promise for a "kinder, gentler nation." Thus, the relationship between government policies and charitable giving is likely to remain of interest in the years to come.

NOTES

1. Salamon and Abramson (1985) estimate that, excluding Medicare and Medicaid, nonprofit organizations lost $49.5 billion in federal government support between 1982 and 1985.

2. For a discussion of free-rider behavior, and its implications, see the seminal work by Olson (1965).

3. The opposite is possible as well. I discuss this in greater detail in Chapter 4.

4. For an important exception, see Menchik and Weisbrod (1987). My work here is, in part, an extension of their research.

5. Hodgkinson and Weitzman (1986), pp. 4, 52.

2.

Charitable Contributions of Money

WHY DO PEOPLE GIVE?

I begin with an analysis of how individuals determine their charitable contributions of money, ignoring volunteer labor for now. I first address the issue of why individuals give and then consider the impact of various government policies on giving.

It is necessary to first define "charitable giving" as used here. I have in mind a broader definition than simply donations that aid the needy. In fact, only a small fraction of giving considered charitable in the legal sense is intended for the poor or otherwise disadvantaged.[1] The U.S. tax code specifies that only a subset of all tax-exempt nonprofit organizations—primarily those exempt under Section 501(c)(3)—are granted tax-deductible status. Contributions to these, and only these, organizations are deductible from the donor's taxable income. We consider charitable giving to include giving to any tax-deductible organization.

This is a useful definition since, to begin with, it underlies most data on charitable giving, at least for the United States. In addition, giving to these, but not other,[2] organizations is directly influenced by tax policy. And, most important, this legal definition of charity seems a reasonable approximation of the economist's notion of a collective, or public, good. That is, organizations that receive tax-deductible status should provide goods and services that generate significant external benefits.

As noted above, the collective nature of charitable output makes private voluntary provision problematic, and government activity potentially desirable. Since I hope to explain the existence of charitable giving, I need to explain both why government is unable to satisfy all its citizens with its public goods provision and why at least some dissatisfied consumers voluntarily contribute rather than free riding.

Government Failure and the Charitable Sector

Although government appears to be the logical locus of provision of collective goods, it is virtually certain that government decisions will leave most citizens dissatisfied with the level of any particular service. Consumers are satisfied with respect to a given good when the price charged to the consumer for that good just equals the benefit he or she receives from the last unit of the good consumed—that is, the marginal benefit of the good just equals its marginal cost.

In a perfectly competitive economy without collective goods, this condition holds for all goods and all consumers. Each individual, lacking control over market prices, simply takes these prices as given and chooses the quantity of each good that equates marginal benefits and costs. However, this condition will generally not hold in the presence of collective goods, for which a single output level is provided, to be consumed by all individuals.[3] In order for all consumers to be satisfied with this single level of output, each must be charged a price—via the tax system—that equates marginal benefit and marginal cost. This is neither feasible—since government would need to know the marginal value placed by each individual on each collective good—nor generally desirable—since it may conflict with other goals of the tax system, such as progressivity.

Following Weisbrod (1975), I call those consumers "undersatisfied" for whom, given their tax share of government output, the private marginal cost of government output is less than the private marginal benefit. That is, given the price they pay for additional government goods and services, undersatisfied consumers would like to see more provided. Those consumers for whom the marginal cost of government output exceeds the marginal benefit are "oversatisfied." Consumers may, of course, be undersatisfied with respect to some government goods and services, oversatisfied with others, and exactly satisfied with yet others.

Dissatisfied consumers have a number of potential actions open to them. They may, for instance, form lobby groups to influence government behavior.[4] Alternatively, they may move to other political jurisdictions with tax-output mixes more to their liking, particularly if the government in question is a state or local one.[5] A third alternative, open to the undersatisfied, but not the oversatisfied, is to supplement the output of collective goods via the charitable sector.

Here, the free-rider problem confronts us. One way to view this problem is to note that the private price of the collective good facing a single donor will be much higher than the price faced as a voter in the political process. A voter may well be undersatisfied with government output, given his or her tax share, but may still not demand any additional output at the high price of financing it privately.

If, for instance, all taxpayers pay an equal tax share, the cost to an individual of one dollar of collective output provided by government is $\$(1/n)$, where n is the total number of taxpayers. The price of financing this output by one's own donation is simply $1 or, if gifts to charity are tax deductible and the donor is an itemizer, $\$(1 - t)$, where t is the marginal tax rate faced by the individual. For any reasonable values of n and t, $(1/n)$ will be much less than $(1 - t)$.

This huge difference between the price to an individual-as-voter and individual-as-donor would seem to lead to the conclusion that only a very small proportion of individuals—those extremely undersatisfied with government output—will give to charity. This does not, however, coincide with the facts. In 1984, for instance, 89 percent of American households contributed some money to charity.[6]

A Partial Explanation of Charitable Giving

It seems likely that my description thus far fails to capture the entire rationale for charitable giving. I have implicitly assumed that charitable output is both identical to that of government and perfectly collective. However, neither of these is likely to be true. For instance, income redistribution carried out by a charity may be very different than that of government welfare programs. A consumer who contributes to charity may pinpoint the type of individual to whom he or she would like income transferred. A donor may choose to redistribute income to the poor in a particular community, or to persons of a particular religion or ethnic group. As a taxpayer, however, an individual cannot make such distinctions about potential recipients.[7] Government is constrained in ways in which charities are not. It may, for instance, "discriminate" by income, but not by religion.

So, for example, if the "good" that a donor is interested in providing is income redistribution to poor Catholics in New Orleans, it may be cheaper for the individual to do so by donating to a charity that serves this specific group rather than relying on government, since only a tiny fraction of income redistribution undertaken by government will reach the desired group. It may, in fact, "pay" for individuals to donate even if they are not undersatisfied with government output since charitable output may be a different good.

In addition, donors may receive a private benefit from giving that cannot be "purchased" by tax payments. A donor may gain satisfaction from the prestige or good reputation that comes with charitable gifts, and this may provide the needed push to induce individuals—who may also have demand for the collective output of charities—to contribute. It is not clear why such satisfaction from giving per se cannot be obtained by voluntarily contributing to government and, in fact, people do contribute to public museums, parks, hospitals and so forth. Very few individuals, however, voluntarily give more in tax payments than they need to.[8] This is likely related to the aforementioned point that dollars donated to the general revenue of the government cannot be earmarked for particular uses.

A MODEL OF "CONDITIONAL DEMAND"[9]

Imagine a single person determining his or her level of charitable giving. Suppose for simplicity that all charities provide a single identical good. The individual chooses an allocation of his or her income between purchases of this charitable good and purchases of private goods. However, because of the collective nature of charitable (and governmental) output, the individual's well-being depends not simply on his or her own decisions, but on the decisions of other donors and of government, over which a single donor has little, if any, control. The more others give, the happier I am, since such gifts by others are costless to me.[10] However, whether increased government output increases my utility depends on whether I am undersatisfied or oversatisfied with the initial level of government production.

Suppose that individuals view their giving decisions as having no effect on the decisions of government or other donors. Each person, then, determines his or her charitable giving—i.e., demand for charitable output—*conditional* on the levels of government output and giving by other donors. This is unlike the demand for private goods, such as chocolate cookies, which is independent of the quantities purchased by other consumers.

There are several parameters of interest in this analysis. First, the extent of free-rider behavior depends on how close a substitute giving by others is for one's own giving.[11] If contributions are motivated only by the desire to increase the output of a single collective good, then own and others' giving are perfect substitutes, and there is little incentive for anyone to give. That is to say, any increase in giving by others will lead to an approximately equal reduction in own giving. The more important are private gains from giving, the poorer substitutes the two are, and the less able one is to free ride on the donations of others.

It is plausible that own and others' donations may be complements, so that increases in giving by other donors will increase giving by any single donor. This would be the case if there are "demonstration effects," so that as donors see others give more, their view of an appropriate level of giving changes.[12] That is, as the level of giving by others increases, it may take larger donations to "buy" prestige and the like via giving, and spending on such goods may rise.

In addition, government output may be either a substitute for or complement of the goods purchased by charitable giving. If governmental and charitable goods are identical, then we might expect cuts in government output to lead to a large—perhaps even dollar-for-dollar—increase in giving, as donors attempt to replace lost government output. This is the notion behind claims that the voluntary sector can compensate for cuts in government social welfare spending. However, as noted above, charitable and governmental goods may be quite different for a number of reasons. It is possible, in fact, that some governmental and charitable goods may be complements, so that cuts in government spending may induce a decrease in giving.

The response of any person to a change in government output will depend not only on the degree of substitutability between charitable and governmental goods, but also whether that person is initially undersatisfied or oversatisfied. Demand for any good, including charitable output, will depend on the level of income— or more generally, well-being—of the consumer. Changes in government output act as increases or decreases in well-being, and so affect the demand for charity. If the consumer is initially over satisfied with the level of government production, any further increase in government output—along with its accompanying cost—will make him or her worse off, while the same increase in output would make an undersatisfied consumer better off.

Thus, a change in government output will affect charitable giving in two conceptually distinct ways—first, via the relationship between governmental and charitable output (the substitution effect) and, second, by changing the level of well-being of individuals who are over or undersatisfied with government output levels (the income effect).

Finally, the prices of charitable and other goods will affect demand for charity, and thus giving. The more expensive charitable output becomes relative to private goods, other things equal, the less charitable output individuals will buy.

With this analytical framework in place, I turn now to examine the impact of tax and spending policies on charitable contributions.

TAX POLICY AND CHARITABLE GIVING

Tax policy can influence charitable giving via both the price of giving and donor income. The income effect of a change in tax policy is straightforward. Any change in tax policy that lowers my disposable income should reduce my giving, other things equal.[13] Even tax policy changes, such as the Tax Reform Act of 1986, that are "revenue neutral"—i.e., that neither raise nor lower the total tax revenue collected—will increase some individuals' incomes while decreasing others. Since individuals differ in the responsiveness of their giving to income changes and in the types of organizations they support, donations will be affected even if aggregate national income is unchanged.

Price effects come about because of the deductibility of charitable contributions. If I itemize on my income tax return, then one dollar contributed to charity saves me t in taxes, where t is my marginal tax rate. Thus, the price of donating one dollar to charity is $\$(1 - t)$. If, however, I do not itemize, the price of giving one dollar is simply $\$1$.[14]

Tax policy can change this price of giving, then, by changing tax rates; any fall in t will tend to reduce giving. (However, the income effect of a tax rate cut will increase giving, so that the net effect is uncertain from theory alone.) In addition, any tax law change that reduces the number of itemizers will tend to reduce contributions by raising the price of giving from $(1 - t)$ to 1 for those taxpayers switching to non-itemizer status. Finally, elimination or reduction in the value of deductibility will depress giving as well. The 1986 Tax Reform Act will reduce charitable contributions for all three of these reasons. (For further discussion of the Tax Reform Act of 1986, see Chapter 9.)

While the impact of taxation on giving has been of interest to economists for at least twenty years,[15] it is only more recently that the relationship between government spending and giving has been closely examined.

THE ROLE OF GOVERNMENT SPENDING: "CROWDING OUT" AND "CROWDING IN"

In the simple model discussed so far, government spending represents production of government output only. (In the next chapter, I allow for government subsidization of the charitable sector.) The question I address here is how a typical donor's demand for charity changes when government output is reduced. This is of particular interest in the context of the debate over whether the voluntary sector compensates for government budget cuts. This question is often posed as "does government spending crowd out charitable giving?" [16]

A cut in government spending will affect an individual's demand for charity in three conceptually distinct ways:

1. by reducing the output of a good, government output, which may be a substitute for or complement of charitable goods and services; other things equal, a decrease in government output will increase demand for charity if the two goods are substitutes and decrease demand for charity if they are complements (the "substitution effect");

2. by affecting giving of other donors (the "donor interaction effect"); and

3. by making the individual better off, if he or she was initially oversatisfied, or worse off, if he or she was undersatisfied (the "income effect").

Proceeding with this analysis, we can determine the conditions under which crowding out will occur, and under which such crowd out will be large or small. If both giving by others and government spending are substitutes for one's own giving (although not necessarily perfect substitutes), and the individual is either satisfied or oversatisfied with government output, then the overall effect of a cut in government spending is to increase demand for charity, and so increase giving. Similarly, an increase in government spending will reduce charitable contributions—that is, crowding out occurs.

We can be certain of the direction of the impact since both the substitution and income effects of the change in government spending work in the same direction. An oversatisfied consumer's well-being increases with a cut in government spending, tending to raise contributions. This reinforces the substitution effect—as the donor attempts to replace lost government output with charity. Other donors will also respond to government cutbacks by increasing their giving[17] and as long as own and others' giving are substitutes, this will reduce own giving—that is, increase free riding. This donor interaction effect will tend to dampen crowding out, but will not eliminate it. (See the Appendix to this chapter for a derivation of this result.)

On the other hand, if giving by others and government spending are each substitutes for one's own giving, but the individual is undersatisfied, a reduction in government spending may increase or decrease contributions; negative crowding out, or "crowding in" may occur. Here the income and substitution effects work in opposite directions; the donor will want to replace the lost government output with charity, but the cut in government spending makes him or her worse off, tending to reduce giving. Whether crowding out or crowding in takes place depends on precisely how undersatisfied the individual is, how responsive giving is to changes in well-being, and how close substitutes government output and giving are.

Results are further complicated if governmental and charitable output are complements. Rose-Ackerman (1986) has argued that this is often the case; as the federal government's role in providing social services expanded through the 1960s and 1970s, charities often attempted to position themselves as complements of government services. For instance, Family Services of America evolved from a provider of relief to an organization whose primary functions are advocacy and representation of the needy before public welfare agencies.

If governmental and charitable outputs are, in fact, complements (but own and others' giving are substitutes), then a cut in government spending will reduce charitable giving by an individual as long as he or she was initially satisfied or undersatisfied. If the donor was initially oversatisfied, the income and substitution effects work in opposite directions, and results are again indeterminate.

"Dollar-for-Dollar" Crowd Out

Several authors[18] have developed theoretical models that generate an extremely strong, and seemingly unrealistic, prediction: each dollar of government spending crowds out exactly one dollar of voluntary giving. Crowd out is complete or dollar for dollar. Such a result has dramatic policy implications. For instance, government would be unable to effectively redistribute income from rich to poor, since any government-imposed transfers will simply be undone by changes in voluntary, charitable, transfers.[19]

The model presented above does not lead to this strong result in general, although it does under certain special conditions. It is useful to spell out those special conditions in order to determine the plausibility of the result. Dollar-for-dollar crowd out will take place if government spending, own giving, and giving by others are perfect substitutes for one another, and if individuals are exactly satisfied with the initial level of government output.[20] For the first assumption, of perfect substitutes, to hold, it must be the case that individuals get no private gain from giving—so that another donor's gift is viewed by me as identical to my own gift—and governmental and charitable outputs must be identical. Neither of these requirements are likely to hold. In fact, if own and others' giving were perfect substitutes, we would expect to find rampant free riding, and virtually no charitable giving.

My analysis predicts that government budget cuts may have very different impacts on donations to different types of charities, depending, in part, on whether these charities provide goods and services that substitute for or complement governmental goods and services and whether these governmental outputs are currently oversupplied or undersupplied from the point of view of donors. Any attempt to find a single impact of government spending on giving will obscure these important differences. Chapter 6 includes an estimate of the extent of crowd out for various types of charities and does, in fact, find important differences.

SUMMARY

This chapter sets out the basic framework with which I analyze charitable donations of money. Within this framework, it can be seen that government tax and spending policies can have important implications for charitable giving. Tax policies affect both the price of giving and the after-tax income of donors, each of which influence donations. Changes in the level of government spending also influence giving, although predicting the direction of the effect is difficult. Claims that significant crowding out occurs are based on certain assumptions, often implicit, that may well not hold.

The analysis thus far has been based on an extremely simple characterization of government, in which its only roles are to collect taxes and produce a single good. I turn now to extend the analysis by allowing for a more realistic description of government activities. In particular, I will incorporate into the analysis the fact that government, in addition to providing goods and services on its own, also subsidizes charitable organizations in their activities. This opens up several important avenues by which government policies can affect the charitable sector.

NOTES

1. Only 8.4 percent of all giving went to organizations that provided social services in 1984, down from 10 percent in 1977. Note, however, that this represents a lower bound on giving to the needy since other categories of giving, such as to religious or health organizations, may also aid the needy. (See Hodgkinson and Weitzman, 1986, p. 117.)

2. Examples of tax-exempt organizations that are not tax deductible include political parties or trade associations.

3. For instance, government can provide only a single level of national defense. Note, however, that individuals need not place the same value on this single quantity.

4. For a discussion of the use of "voice" as a reaction to consumer dissatisfaction, see Hirschman (1970).

5. Tiebout (1956) provides the seminal analysis of this process.

6. Hodgkinson and Weitzman (1986), p. 6.

7. I ignore, for now, the issue of how much information the donor actually has about who receives his or her donation.

8. The Internal Revenue Service (IRS) does maintain an account for "gifts" to reduce the national debt. In 1982, this account received $901,136 in donations. The IRS estimates that one in 25,000 taxpayers makes such a donation. (See "Some Loyal Americans Bring Down the National Debt by $135,575.15," *Wall Street Journal*, April 1, 1983, p. 15).

9. The mathematics of this model is presented in the Appendix to this chapter. For a similar model, see Steinberg (1987).

10. I ignore, for now, the possibility that charitable output may be a "bad" for me. For example, donations to a fundamentalist religious school may make an atheist worse off.

11. Two goods are substitutes if an increase in the price of one increases the quantity demanded of the other. Goods are complements if an increase in the price of one leads to a decrease in the quantity demanded of the other. Loosely speaking, substitutes tend to replace one another in consumption, while complements are used together.

12. See Feldstein and Clotfelter (1976) for a discussion of demonstration effects.

13. This assumes that charitable output is a normal good, i.e., a good the demand for which increases with income. This is the case for most, but not all, goods.

14. The 1981 Economic Recovery Tax Act allowed for a phasing in of a charitable deduction for non-itemizers. However, this was dropped in the 1986 Tax Reform Act.

15. For a review of the empirical literature, see Clotfelter (1985).

16. See, e.g., Abrams and Schmitz (1978, 1984), Schiff (1985), and Steinberg (1987).

17. This assumes that other donors also view governmental and charitable output as substitutes and are oversatisfied or satisfied.

18. See Warr (1982) and Roberts (1984) for models that predict complete crowd out. For a more general model similar to the one presented here, see Steinberg (1987).

19. This is the case as long as giving is greater than zero. Once giving reaches zero, no further reductions are possible, so that government transfers will not be offset.

20. Alternatively, the income effects on consumers could cancel out, so that in the aggregate only the substitution effect remains.

Appendix: Derivation of Conditional Demand Results

Each individual maximizes his or her utility, $U(y, z_1, z_2, z_3)$, subject to:

$$I - y - p_1 z_1 - p_2 z_2 = 0 \qquad (1)$$

$$z_1 - z_1{}^* = 0, \text{ and} \qquad (2)$$

$$z_3 - z_3{}^* = 0 \qquad (3)$$

where y is a private good, z_1 is government output, z_2 is charitable output financed by own donations, and z_3 is charitable output fianced by donations of others. The exogenous levels of z_1 and z_3 are represented by $z_1{}^*$ and $z_3{}^*$ respectively. The individual's income is I, and p_1 and p_2 are the prices, to the individual, of z_1 and z_2.

The conditional demand 1/ function for z_2--i.e. demand given $z_1{}^*$ and $z_3{}^*$--can be written as:

$$z_2 = z_2(p_1, p_2, I, z_1{}^*, z_3{}^*) \qquad (4)$$

The change in demand for charity, z_2, due to a change in government output, z_1, holding giving by others, z_3, fixed, can be expreassed as: 2/

$$\frac{\partial z_2}{\partial z_1}\Big|_{z_3} = \frac{\partial z_2{}^u}{\partial z_1{}^*} - \frac{\partial z}{\partial I}\left[\frac{\partial y^u}{\partial z_1{}^*} + p_2\frac{\partial z_2{}^u}{\partial z_1{}^*} + p_1\right] \qquad (5)$$

where $z_2{}^u$ and y^u are demands for z_2 and y with utility fixed at some level U^*.

Note that $\partial z_2{}^u/\partial z_1{}^*$ is the change in demand for z_2 due to a change in z_1, holding utility constant. This term is negative if z_1 and z_2 are substitutes (equal to -1 if perfect substitutes) and positive if they are complements.

The term in brackets represents the impact on income of increased z_1--the difference between the cost to the individual of an extra unit of z_1, namely p_1, and the benefit he or she receives from that unit, $\partial y^u/\partial z_1{}^* + p_2[\partial z_2{}^u/\partial z_1{}^*]$. This term is the amount by which the consumer could decrease spending on y and z_2, following an increase in z_1, and still remain as well off as before the change; that is, it equals the marginal benefit of z_1. If the expression in brackets is negative, the consumer is undersatisfied, and the income effect--the term in brackets multiplied by $(-\partial z_2/\partial I)$--is positive (assuming z_2 is a normal good). If the expression in brackets is positive, the individual is oversatisfied and the income effect is negative.

The results of Section III are easily obtained from (5). If, for instance, z_1 and z_2 are perfect substitutes and there is no income effect, we would predict "dollar-for-dollar" crowdout.

The overall impact of government spending on contributions, i.e. allowing giving by others to change, is:

$$\frac{\partial z_2}{\partial z_1^*} = \frac{\partial z_2}{\partial z_1^*}\Big|_{z_3} + \frac{\partial z_2}{\partial z_3}\frac{\partial z_3^*}{\partial z_1^*} \tag{6}$$

If all individuals are identical, we can write:

$$\frac{\partial z_3^*}{\partial z_1^*} = (n-1)\frac{\partial z_2}{\partial z_1^*} \tag{7}$$

where n is the total number of individuals. Plugging (7) into (6) and rearranging terms, we have:

$$\frac{\partial z_2}{\partial z_1} = \frac{(\partial z_2/\partial z_1^*)|_{z_3}}{1-(n-1)(\partial z_2/\partial z_3)} \tag{8}$$

As long as $\partial z_2/\partial z_3 < 0$, then $\partial z_2/\partial z_1^*$ will have the same sign as $(\partial z_2/\partial z_1^*)|_{z_3}$. So, for instance, if z_1, z_2 and z_3 are all perfect substitutes for each individual, and there is no income effect, then (8) equals $(1/n)$, so that each dollar increase in z_1 crowds out $(1/n)$ dollars per individual, or one dollar in total.

Footnotes

1/ See Pollack (1969) for a general discussion of conditional demand functions.

2/ For a derivation, see Mackay and Whitney (1980).

3.

Government Grants and Charitable Giving

EXTENDING THE MODEL: THE ROLE OF GRANTS

Government finances charitable provisions of goods and services both directly, via grants and purchases of service and indirectly, by providing numerous tax[1] and other advantages.[2] In fact, direct government support accounted for 27 percent of non-profit revenue in 1984, the same percentage as private contributions.[3] The introduction of this role for government complicates the analysis by providing additional avenues via which government policies may influence giving.

I will argue that the impact of government spending cuts (or increases) on charitable giving depends in part on the extent to which those cuts represent reductions in the government's own production of goods and services as opposed to cuts in government support for the charitable sector. The overall impact on the charitable sector of a change in spending policy will reflect both the direct impact of that policy on government support received, and any induced change in giving. In general, both the total resources available to the charitable sector and the distribution of the resources between public and private sources will be affected by government spending policies, and each may have important consequences.

Suppose, to begin with, that government subsidies to the charitable sector are grants made with "no strings attached." That is, government provides the subsidy without constraining the behavior of the recipient organization in any way. In this case, the receipt of a grant by a charity is viewed by each individual donor as equivalent to an increase in giving by others. Output financed by government grants is identical to output financed by increased private giving.

It seems reasonable to assume that output financed by one's own charitable gift to an organization is a closer substitute for output financed by a grant—or, equivalently, by others' gifts to that organization—than it is for government produced output. If this is the case, a cut in government grants will crowd out more charitable giving than a cut in government production, as there will be more incentive for donors to attempt to replace the lost output. So, for instance, one might expect a cut in government's arts budget to increase donations relatively sharply since such cuts will almost exclusively reflect reductions in grants to the charitable sector. On the other hand, such budgets cuts will have a negative and dramatic direct impact on public revenues received by such charitable arts organizations.

This analysis, while a good starting point, omits several crucial facts.[4] First, government support may require charities to alter the nature of their output. This change in the types of goods and services provided will influence donations, apart from the impact of any changes in the level of output. Charities accepting large subsidies will, in the extreme, become a de facto part of government. Whether this "governmentalization" of charities encourages or discourages private giving is an open question, which is discussed later.

Second, a large grant from government may allow a charity to significantly increase its scale of operation. If the larger scale makes the organization more efficient—able to produce charitable output more cheaply—then government support of nonprofit organizations will tend to encourage donations.

Finally, government support of a charitable organization may provide information to donors about that organization. It may, for instance, act as a "seal of approval," indicating that the charity is of a quality that the government has found acceptable. This point will be addressed in the next chapter, when I consider the implications of imperfect information for the analysis.

GRANTS AND CONSTRAINTS

When a charity accepts a government grant, or purchase-of-service offer, it often finds itself constrained to carry out a particular program that may differ significantly from its initial one, and it may also be forced to accept government monitoring of its activities. In a survey of charities in the Greater New York United Way (Hartogs, 1978), for instance, 56 percent of those organizations receiving government funding stated that their funded program was "different, but related" to their original program, and 5 percent said that the funded program was "completely different." In addition, one-third of the charities claimed that as a result of accepting government funding their program's target population had changed.

How does this implicit regulation of the charitable sector influence charitable giving? In order to attempt to answer this question, I drop the assumption that all charities produce identical output.

Heterogeneous Charities

Suppose that charitable organizations may differ in two ways.[5] First, they may differ in their level of efficiency, so that some charities are able to produce a unit of charitable output more cheaply than others. Second, they may differ in the type of output produced. To simplify, suppose that "type" varies only by the amount of a single characteristic, denoted by q, per unit of output.[6]

The satisfaction a potential donor receives from a unit of output of a given organization depends on how close the organization's output type, q, is to his or her preferred type.[7] The smaller is this deviation, other things equal, the more the donor will give to a charity. So, whether an individual donor increases or decreases giving to a charity after it accepts government support[8] depends, in part, on whether the new q is closer to or further from his or her preferred type.

If, for instance, the output in question is child care, q might refer to the educational philosophy espoused by a child care center. Donors will prefer to give to a provider whose philosophy closely matches their own. In fact, if the philosophy espoused by a provider is sufficiently different from that preferred by a donor, increased output by that center could make the individual worse off. An atheist, for instance, may be made worse off by increased enrollment in a fundamentalist Christian child care program.

Government grants to a child care program might be accompanied by requirements that children of all religious backgrounds be admitted, that a certain curriculum be taught, and so forth. This would make the program more attractive to some potential donors and less attractive to others. In order to say more about the impact of government grants on private giving, it is necessary to know how the initial output type is chosen, and the conditions under which a constraining grant would be accepted by a charity.

Grants, Output Type, and Donations

In the absence of any government constraints, each charity chooses its own value of q. It does not do so in a vacuum, however. All charities need revenue to survive, so they must take into account the distribution of donor preferences over q. The q that is chosen will typically be neither that type which the charitable manager[9] would most prefer, nor that which maximizes donations. Rather, the choice of q will represent a compromise between the two.

I assume that the charitable manager cares about both the revenue of the organization and the type of output produced. (Special cases will be considered in which the manager cares only about one or the other of these.) The manager may care about total revenue for several reasons. First, running a large charitable organization may imply greater power, prestige, and income than running a smaller one. So, a purely self-interested manager may attempt to maximize revenues.[10] However, an altruistic manager may also desire to maximize revenues since a larger budget will allow the organization to increase its output and serve a larger clientele.

The manager also cares about the type of output produced by the organization and may be unwilling to increase revenues at the expense of moving q too far from its preferred value. A fundamentalist Christian child care program may not drop its ideology simply to increase donations. The choice of output type reflects a compromise between the preferences of the charity and those of potential donors.

When Are Grants Worth It?

Suppose that government has some preferred output type, which we denote by q_G, and that any government grant to a charity requires that charity to move its q closer to q_G.[11] Imagine that the charity is offered a grant of S dollars, contingent on moving q closer to q_G by some stated amount. The acceptance of such a grant would have both benefits and costs for the charity. While it would, other things equal, allow the organization to expand, it may adversely affect private giving and constrain the organization to produce a mix of goods and services that—at least from the charity's point of view—is less desirable.

To simplify, assume that there are only two sources of revenue for a charity—government grants, denoted by G, and private contributions, C.[12] Ignore for now the role of solicitations and view both types of revenue as simply being offered to the charity, which may accept it or not. A grant will be accepted by the charity if and only if the combination of changes in total revenue—from government and private giving—and output type are viewed by the charity as a net gain. Private giving is affected by grants in two ways. First, the receipt of a grant allows a charity to increase its output, which tends to crowd out private giving. In addition, the grant will influence q, further influencing private contributions.

Insight can be gained into the charity's decision to accept a grant or not by looking at two special cases. First, suppose that charitable managers were completely dedicated to producing a particular type of output, so that no trade-off between q and total revenue would be accepted. In this case, the initial (without the grant) choice of q would simply be that value most preferred by the manager, and no grant would be accepted that affected this q. Unless, however, the q chosen allowed significant revenues to be raised, such an ideologically pure charity would not exist for long.

If, at the other extreme, managers act solely as budget maximizers—so that output type is irrelevant to them—then a grant would be accepted as long as it increases total revenue, i.e., as long as any induced fall in private donations is more than compensated for by the new grant revenue. Only in this case will private giving necessarily fall with the receipt of a grant, since the initial choice of q maximized private giving. The fall in donations must, however, be less than the grant, since the grant would not be accepted otherwise.

It seems likely that the typical charity cares both about q and total revenue. Many organizations actively pursue government support despite the constraints such support implies, suggesting that charities are generally not ideologically pure. On the other hand, we would not expect huge shifts in goods and services provided in return for modest gains in revenue. It is interesting to note that, in this general case, a grant may be accepted even if total revenue falls as a result—that is, even if private giving falls by more than the size of the grant. A manager may, in the absence of grants, be forced to choose a q very different from his or her preferred value, in order to generate revenue from private donors. Moving away from this q toward q_G may actually move the manager closer to his or her preferred value, and this may outweigh any loss in revenue.

Any one charity's choice of q depends on the choices made by other charities as well. Each organization attempts to find its niche in the market so that if many charities are clustered near a particular q, it may pay for others to move away from that q, even if such a move represents a move away from one's own preferred value. A grant-induced change in q of one charity may, similarly, influence giving to many organizations. If, for example, the receipt of a grant by a formerly Christian fundamentalist child care provider causes the provider to shed its religious orientation and donations to the organization to fall, we might expect some former donors to increase giving to other religious child care providers. Thus, any fall in contributions to the charity receiving the grant will likely exceed the reduction in aggregate giving.

In the longer run, government grants may also stimulate entry into the charitable sector as organizations form in response to the possibility of receiving government support. This appears to have occurred in response to the increase in government social welfare spending associated with the War on Poverty. (See Chapter 8 for a discussion of this point.)

Grants and the Efficiency of Charities

We have focused thus far on the impact of government support on the type of charitable output provided. However, such support may affect the efficiency of charitable operations as well, and the impact on efficiency of a nonprofit charity may be quite different than if the firm in question operated for profit.

Nonprofit organizations are constrained to use all profits to purchase additional inputs. Specifically, profits may not be distributed to owners, who may earn only reasonable compensation. This nondistribution constraint[13] may imply a lack of incentive to produce efficiently, so we might expect waste in the production of charitable output. Government could reduce this waste by monitoring the activities of a supported organization, partially filling the role of an entrepreneur in a for-profit firm.

However, government monitoring will not, in all likelihood, prove effective in enhancing efficiency. Government regulators are, after all, similar to nonprofit managers in that neither is allowed to appropriate firm profits. Thus, the same incentive problem that caused the initial inefficiency will limit the impact of regulation. In fact, it is quite plausible that efficiency could fall—i.e., costs could rise—with government support since administrative costs of compliance with government reporting requirements, for instance, could rise substantially. Hartogs (1978) estimates that administrative costs associated with a government grant average 27.2 percent of the grant.

Government support may also affect the efficiency of a charity's operation by increasing its size, either allowing the charity to take advantage of economies of scale,[14] or by pushing the firm into a range of diseconomies.

Suppose that the net effect of government support is to increase efficiency. How will individual giving be affected? Facing a lower price for charitable output, donors should increase their demand for that output. This may, however, increase or decrease contributions to that charity, depending on the elasticity of demand for charity by donors. If demand is inelastic—so that donors demand approximately the same quantity of output regardless of price—giving could actually fall, since donors could finance the same amount of charity while giving less. It seems more likely, however, that the demand for the output of any single charity would be quite price elastic, since a fall in price would attract donors who had been giving to other similar organizations. Thus, enhanced efficiency should increase donations received, although this increase will come, at least in part, at the expense of other charities.

SUMMARY

Government finances the provision of charitable goods and services by providing grants and purchases of service, and by granting tax and other advantages. Changes in the level of government support for charitable organizations will influence private giving both via the simple crowd-out route, discussed in Chapter 2, but also by influencing the mix of goods and services provided by charitable organizations and the efficiency with which those goods and services are produced.

In the next chapter, I supplement this analysis by considering the role of government support of charities in a world of imperfect information.

NOTES

1. Nonprofit organizations are exempt from federal and most state corporate income taxes as well as most state and local property taxes.

2. For instance, nonprofits enjoy lower postal rates.

3. Hodgkinson and Weitzman (1986), p. 32. The remainder of revenue comes primarily from sales and investment income.

4. See Rose-Ackerman (1987) and Schiff and Weisbrod (1986) for a discussion of the impact of government grants on charitable organizations.

5. This section is based, in part, on Rose-Ackerman (1987).

6. Alternatively, "type" can be thought of as varying in two dimensions, with q a ratio of the two.

7. I assume that each individual has preferences over q that are "single peaked," so that any movement of q toward an individual's most preferred value makes him or her better off.

8. I refer to government support hereafter as "grants" although it may also take the form of purchase-of-service contracts.

9. I treat the charity as if it has a single decision-making manager. In truth, many charities are run by boards of directors.

10. Niskanen (1975) models the behavior of a government bureaucrat as a budget maximizer for similar reasons.

11. I assume also that q moves continuously closer to q_G as the size of the grant increases.

12. I ignore sales revenue here. For such a discussion, see Schiff and Weisbrod (1986).

13. See Hansmann (1980) for a discussion of the nondistribution constraint.

14. Rose-Ackerman (1986) makes this point.

4.

Giving, Imperfect Information, and Government Policies

INTRODUCTION

I have assumed to this point that donors have perfect information about the behavior of charitable organizations. In particular, each individual has been assumed to know how much output is financed by his or her contribution, as well as the type of output produced. In reality, however, donors are often unable, or able only at great cost, to observe or evaluate the benefits resulting from their gifts and this, in fact, may explain why charities take on the nonprofit legal form.

In this chapter, I consider the implications of imperfect donor information for the analysis thus far. First, I discuss the nature of the information problem in the market for charity. Next, I describe the ways in which both sides of the market—charities and donors—have responded to the problem. Finally, I examine ways in which government policies may provide information to donors, and so influence giving.

CHARITY AND ASYMMETRIC INFORMATION

There are many goods—charitable and other—about which consumers have poor information and, in particular, have less information than producers. Think, for instance, about the typical consumer's problem in choosing a used car.[1] However, the collective nature of charitable goods and services suggests that asymmetric information is a particularly important problem for the charitable sector.

A good may be collective either because of its technological characteristics or because of the nature of consumer preferences, particularly toward the persons ultimately consuming the good. In either case, a donor is likely to suffer from a lack of information, although for somewhat different reasons.

Take public radio as an example of the first type of collective good. A contribution to a public radio station that finances one hour of radio time provides a benefit for all listeners, not simply the donor. However, it is difficult, if not impossible, for the donor to determine whether his or her contribution has led to any increase in the quantity or quality of air time or whether the station manager has simply pocketed the gift. The donor does not know the marginal impact of his or her donation since it is impossible to ascertain what the quantity and quality of air time would have been in the absence of the gift. That is, the donor does not know the efficiency with which donations are turned into output, although the type of output, q, can be readily observed by listening to the station.

If public radio stations excluded listeners who did not pay a monthly charge (as do cable T.V. stations), the information problem would not exist. Each subscriber would know precisely what he or she was purchasing—the ability to listen to public radio for one month. The marginal impact of paying the monthly fee is clearcut since, in the absence of the payment, no public radio could be consumed by the individual.

For the second source of collectiveness, consumer preferences, the information problem is at least as severe. In this case, it is the nature of the recipient, rather than technology, that gives the good its collective nature. Here donors will tend to be poorly informed about both efficiency and output type.

Take, for instance, the organization CARE, which provides food to the needy in less developed countries.[2] If a donor finances the shipment of food to the needy, he or she is providing a collective good, assuming others value the recipient's consumption of food. Food consumed by the non-needy, however, will likely not be collective to any significant degree.

Whenever the recipient of the output is someone other than the individual paying for it—here the donor—it will be costly for the payer to learn whether the output ever reached its intended recipient and, if it did, what its quality was. In the case of CARE, the donor never observes the output and so is uncertain about both efficiency and output type.

Responses to Asymmetric Information

Donors and charities have each responded in various ways to information problems in the charity market. However, certain responses—such as warranties or guarantees—that are effective for private goods, may be of little use for charitable goods, since those devices rely on the consumer learning about the goods after purchase. Donors may never receive the information required.

Donors have attempted to overcome their position of informational inferiority in a number of ways. First, they may—despite the costs involved—search for information. I argue, in the next chapter, that this search provides an important motive for volunteering.

Second, donors may take certain observable characteristics of a charity as indicators of the unobservable quality. They may, for instance, view the age or size of an organization as a proxy for quality, believing that the success reflected by larger, longer lived organizations is a result of giving by more well-informed donors.[3] In a similar manner, donors may take the receipt of a government grant as an indicator of the quality of a charity; more on this below.

Finally, donors may respond to their inability to observe firm quality by attempting to constrain a charity's use of their donations. For instance, a donor may give money to a university to build a gymnasium, rather than to its general operating fund. Such contraints may not be effective, however. Earmarking funds for a gymnasium may simply free up resources that would otherwise have been used to build a gymnasium for some other purposes; the marginal effect of the gift, then, might be very different than that intended by the donor.

Volunteering rather than giving money may also serve as a constraint on charitable organizations. Donating time is equivalent to giving money with the constraint that it be used to hire the individual volunteering. Again, however, the marginal impact of volunteering may be very different than the apparent impact, if the donated time simply frees resources that would have been used to pay for an hour of labor.[4]

Charitable organizations also attempt to deal with the information problems in a variety of ways. Charities voluntarily constrain themselves by taking on the nonprofit form in order to encourage giving.[5] The nondistribution constraint limits the uses to which profits may be put—in particular, they may not be distributed to firm owners. This provides a certain assurance to donors that their gifts are at least used to provide goods and services, rather than ending up in the pocket of the manager of the charity, although it does not provide information about the type of output provided, or the efficiency with which it is produced. Note, too, that enforcement of the nondistribution constraint is costly, so that cheating is possible.

Membership in a united charity (UC), such as United Way, may provide further assurance to donors about the trustworthiness of an organization.[6] Because exploitative behavior by one member of a UC will, if discovered, reduce donations to all members, charities in a UC have incentive to monitor one another. Knowing this, donors may be more willing to contribute.

Finally a charity may provide information about its activities in order to convince potential donors that the organization is of high quality. Charities typically solicit contributions, providing information in the process. In the next section, I consider how charities decide whether, and how much, to solicit.

SOLICITATIONS AND CONTRIBUTIONS

Although potential donors are typically uncertain about the quality—efficiency and output type—of charitable organizations, they will have some "best guess" about these characteristics. These beliefs, or expectations, will influence giving: the more efficient a donor believes a charity to be and the closer the organization's q is thought to be to the donor's preferred value, the more, other things being equal, he or she will contribute.

In addition to expectations, the degree of certainty with which a donor's beliefs are held may also influence giving. A donor would prefer to give to a charity he or she knows with certainty to be of high quality than one he or she merely expects to be of high quality.[7] Since certainty has value to donors, it follows that one may prefer to give to an organization about which one knows a great deal rather than give to a largely unknown organization, even if one's best guess is that the little-known organization is of higher quality.

Donors are not the only agents with imperfect information. Managers of charities are also uncertain about a key parameter—the preferences of potential donors regarding q. (All donors would prefer greater efficiency.) I assume that each manager also has a best guess about these preferences, which may be based on several types of information. First, the manager may know that a donor has contributed to the organization in the past. This indicates that the individual has preferred q near that of the charity, or at least near its past q. The manager may also be able to obtain information about donations to other charities by purchasing or trading mailing lists. Finally, just knowing an individual's address or occupation may provide information about likely ethnic background, income, or educational attainment, which may provide the charity with some basis for inferring their q.

Since the manager has some information about donor preferences, he or she need not provide costly information in a random fashion but can direct it to those individuals who seem most likely to respond by contributing. The organization may provide information about efficiency and/or output type, but I assume that the information provided must be accurate. Information regarding efficiency is often couched in terms of the percentage of income that goes toward producing output, as opposed to administrative and solicitation expenses.[8]

Information provided by solicitations can influence contributions either by changing donor expectations about organization quality or by making donors more certain of their expectations.[9]

It will typically do both. Suppose that a charity provides information about q to a potential donor. The fact that the donor is now more certain about q will tend to increase his or her giving to the organization. On the other hand, information will lead a donor to change his or her expectation of q, moving it either toward or away from the preferred value. If the solicitation causes the consumer to move his expectation of the firm's q closer to his own, giving to that organization will increase.[10] Even, however, if the solicitation moves the donor's expectation of the charity's q further from his or her own, giving may still rise because the increased certainty brought about may offset at least small disappointments regarding q. Solicitations that provide information about efficiency will affect giving in a similar fashion. Both the expectation of efficiency and the certainty with which that expectation is held will be affected.

The Optimal Level of Solicitations

Given that solicitations are costly but will increase donations, how is the optimal level of solicitation expenditures determined by a charity? Since a charity's manager has some information about potential donors, he or she will first solicit donations from the most "promising" ones—i.e., those from whom the manager expects to receive the largest donations in response. As solicitations increase, they will either reach increasingly less promising donors—such as those with preferred values of q far from the organization's choice—or will simply represent second and third attempts to reach more promising donors. In either case, we would expect that contributions will eventually begin to rise at a decreasing rate as solicitation expenditures increase.

Some contributions will be forthcoming, for the typical charity, without any solicitations. As a charity begins to solicit, there are likely to be significant setup costs involved, such as hiring a fundraiser. Once the solicitation program is in place, donations may rise rapidly to the initial solicitations. As solicitations grow, however, charities will eventually experience diminishing returns to additional solicitations.

How much will a charity spend on solicitations? This depends on the manager's objectives. However, if the manager wishes to maximize donations net of solicitations—which is consistent with a number of plausible underlying objective functions, including those discussed in Chapter 3—the charity will continue to solicit as long as a dollar spent on solicitations raises at least one dollar in donations. The optimal level of solicitation expenditures is, therefore, either the level at which the last dollar of solicitations raises just one dollar in donations, or zero solicitations, if sufficient donations are received without soliciting.

DONORS, GOVERNMENT POLICIES, AND INFORMATION

Now that I have described the various ways in which donors and charities deal with the problem of asymmetric information, I turn to an analysis of the role that government plays in providing information, and so influencing charitable giving. These information avenues via which government affects giving exist in addition to those discussed for a world of perfect information.

Government policies may provide information to donors in two basic ways. First, government grants, which are typically accompanied by constraints on and monitoring of charitable organizations, allow increased donor certainty. Second, even if government does not actually affect a charity's behavior at all, financial support of the organization may act as a "seal of approval," indicating that the charity has met some quality standard.

Constraints and Donor Certainty

The analysis in Chapter 3 supported the contention that government grants can affect both the efficiency of an organization and the type of output it produces, and that these changes influence charitable giving. That analysis stands in a world of imperfect information as well, with one addition. Now, such grant-induced changes also influence giving by affecting both donors' expectations of efficiency and output type and the certainty with which those expectations are held. Because donors value certainty, introducing this new element appears to make it more likely that government grants will encourage private donations.

The "Seal of Approval"

Government support of a charitable organization may act as a signal to potential donors, independent of any real change that it may bring about in the charity's behavior. When government provides a grant to a charity, it may be taken as a proxy for either efficiency or output type.

The donor may view the support received as evidence that efficiency is at least equal to some (perhaps implicit) government standard. That is, the donor may assume, rightly or wrongly, that the government has itself gathered information about the efficiency of the charity and found it acceptable. It was noted above that donors may take the fact that others have contributed to some charity as evidence of its quality. The role of government is simply a special case of that, with the "other donor" here being the government.

The value of a seal of approval will be greater the higher donors believe government standards to be, and the less efficient they initially (before government support) believed the charity to be. If the donors already believed that charity was of high quality and that government standards were low, receiving government support would have little impact on contributions, beyond that already discussed for the perfect information case. If, however, donors initially believed a charity to be very inefficient, and viewed government standards as strict, then government support could have a large impact on donations received, independent of any impact government spending might have on the actual efficiency of the charity. In any case, it seems unlikely that government support would be viewed as an unfavorable signal about firm efficiency, unless donors believe that government prefers to support inefficient organizations. Recall that any seal-of-approval effects of government support are in addition to any impact such support may have on the true efficiency of a charity.

Government grants to a charity may also be taken as an indicator of the organization's output type. Consumers may believe that government has learned about a charity's q before deciding to support it, so that a grant may be viewed as evidence that q is close to that preferred by government, q_G. This information may encourage or discourage donations, depending on the distribution of donor preferences regarding q. Again, this effect is separate from any influence government support may actually have on q.

Therefore, whether government support acts, on net, as a seal of approval, encouraging donations, or of disapproval, reducing gifts, depends on:

1. donors' initial beliefs about the efficiency of the charity;
2. the minimum standard of efficiency that donors believe an organization must meet before being considered for government grants;
3. donors' initial beliefs about the type of output produced by the charity, q;
4. the distribution of donor preferences over q.

If consumers have a low regard for government—in the sense both that they believe that the government's minimum efficiency standard is low and that they have a preferred q far from q_G— then the receipt of a government grant may actually decrease giving to an organization.

As in the perfect information case, any change in giving to a particular organization may come, in part, from changes in giving to other charities. So, if government support of one private social welfare agency acts as a seal of approval for that agency, donors may divert their giving from other similar organizations to the supported charity. The increase (or decrease) in giving to a single grant recipient will, therefore, exceed the increase (decrease) in aggregate giving.

On the other hand, support for a particular charity may act as a seal of approval, not just for that organization, but for all organizations engaged in similar activities. For instance, government support for one cancer group may be viewed by donors as an indication that cancer research, in general, has a high "payoff" to society. Thus, the grant-supported cancer research group may benefit at the expense not of other cancer research groups but, rather, of charities in competing fields, such as research into heart disease.

Solicitations and Government Grants

Government support of charitable organizations may, by providing information about those organizations to potential donors, reduce the incentive for charities to provide information by soliciting. In the extreme, government support would provide all relevant information, so that solicitations would have no effect on contributions, and solicitation expenditures would fall to zero. In reality, solicitations will not completely duplicate the information implicit in government support. However, as long as the marginal effect of solicitations on giving is reduced by grants, solicitation expenditures will fall, although not necessarily to zero.

In fact, any policy that affects giving can influence the level of solicitations, whether that policy provides information or not. A cut in the level of government output, for instance, will (as long as governmental and charitable output are substitutes) cause contributions to rise at any level of solicitation spending. Whether such an increase leads to a rise or fall in solicitations depends, however, on whether the marginal impact of a dollar spent on soliciting increases or decreases. Anecdotal evidence suggests that the initial round of Reagan budget cuts increased the marginal effectiveness of soliciting, raising such expenditures by somewhere on the order of one-third.[11] Such an increase would increase giving, strengthening the direct impact of cuts in government output. However, only the increase in giving net of solicitations would be available to provide charitable goods and services.

SUMMARY

Once we account for the fact that charitable markets are often characterized by imperfect donor information, we are able to better explain various features of these markets. Volunteering, solicitations, united charities, and the nonprofit legal form are all, in part, responses to information problems.

In addition, the existence of asymmetric information opens up several new avenues for government to influence charitable giving. Government support of a charity provides information about the efficiency and output type of the recipient organization, affecting donations. Such support may also influence solicitation decisions, further influencing private giving.

NOTES

1. Akerlof (1970), using used cars as an example, shows that asymmetric information will reduce the size of a market, and perhaps eliminate it.

2. Hansmann (1980) uses this example.

3. Weisbrod and Dominguez (1986) find that older organizations do, in fact, have an easier time raising funds.

4. Volunteers may not consider this possibility. In the *National Survey of Philanthropy* (1974), volunteers were asked, "If you gave money instead, would the organization pay someone to do the work, or would they still rely on volunteers?" Over 80 percent responded that the organization would still rely on volunteers, compared with 7 percent who thought someone would be hired. (The remainder were uncertain.)

5. There are other possible reasons why an organization may seek nonprofit status, e.g., the tax advantages gained by doing so.

6. See Rose-Ackerman (1980) for an economic analysis of a united charity.

7. This will be true if the donor is risk averse.

8. Steinberg (1986) argues that such a measure of efficiency is inappropriate. The appropriateness of the measure, however, is a separate issue from whether or not donors care about it.

9. Solicitations may also make the donor aware of the existence of a charity. This may be seen as an extreme case of increased certainty of quality.

10. Or at least not decrease. For most pairs of individuals and charities, giving is zero.

11. *New York Times*, December 12, 1982, p. 48 ("Charity Appeals Sharply on the Rise") quotes Thomas Sanberg, chairman of the board of the National Society of Fundraising Executives as saying, "Fundraising activity has exploded in the last 18 months. We estimate at least one-third more soliciting is going on."

5.

An Economic Analysis of
Volunteering

INTRODUCTION

In Chapters 2 through 4, I analyzed charitable donations of money, largely ignoring contributions of time, or volunteer labor. However, volunteer labor represents an extremely important resource of nonprofit organizations, comparable in value to donations of money. In 1984, approximately $80 billion worth of time was donated to charitable organizations, compared with $73 billion of money contributions. Any examination of the impact of government policies on the charitable sector should, therefore, consider the potential effects of such policies on the amount of time, or labor, donated.

In addition to the quantitative significance of donations of time, there are other good reasons to study volunteer behavior. Even if one is primarily interested in understanding donations of money, volunteering should nevertheless be studied; analyzing the donor's choice between contributing money and time provides insight into the motivations for each type of giving. I will present evidence that money and time are given for quite different reasons and that while government policies influence both types of giving, they do so in very different ways.

Finally, a number of issues that arise in examining volunteer behavior are of more general interest. For instance, the ability of volunteers to acquire job skills has implications for the functioning of wage labor markets.

My primary interests in this chapter are to explain why individuals volunteer—and especially why they do so rather than give money—and to analyze the impact of various government policies on the decision to volunteer. I begin by arguing that the model developed for money donations in previous chapters is not sufficient to explain volunteering. In particular, it is difficult to explain why tax itemizers would ever volunteer, or why some donors give both money and time to charity.

A number of alternative models of volunteering are presented, none of which tells the whole story. I consider the possibility, first, that volunteering provides a private benefit, such as membership in a "club," that contributions of money cannot. Next, I model volunteer behavior as being motivated by a desire for influence over, or information about, the activities of an organization. A final explanation—that people volunteer as a means of acquiring job skills—is also considered.

THE "COLLECTIVE GOODS" MODEL REVISITED

I begin by returning to the simple model of Chapter 2. There I assumed that charitable contributions result from the demand for charitable output, a good about which consumers were assumed to have perfect information. The question addressed here is whether volunteering can be adequately understood within this model.

Why Volunteer?

If donors wish only to finance charitable output, it is not clear why they would prefer to give time rather than money, since money donations are likely to represent a less costly means of finance. To see this, imagine an individual choosing between donating money and time. If a donor volunteers an hour of time, the cost he or she incurs is the value of that hour in its next best alternative use—the opportunity cost of time. If labor markets are functioning smoothly, there are no taxes, and individuals can freely choose the number of hours they wish to work for pay—clearly rather big "ifs"—this opportunity cost will equal the individual's wage rate, since each person will allocate his or her time to equate the marginal value of time in all its uses. Let's refer to this wage rate as w.[1]

The value of the donated hour to the recipient organization will, however, be less than w, since w represents the maximum wage the individual could earn—i.e., the most productive use of his or her time. We would expect people to be more productive in their paid jobs than as volunteers. I refer to the value to the organization of an hour volunteered as w^*, which will be less—and possibly a good deal less—than w.

The donor could, rather than volunteer an hour, contribute w dollars, and incur the same cost of w. These w dollars will have a value to the organization of w, since the dollars can be used to purchase any inputs. Since $w > w^*$, an individual could do better by giving money rather than time. One way to look at this is to view a contribution of time as a constrained gift. By volunteering one hour, a donor is, in effect, giving w dollars to the organization, with the constraint that the organization must use that money to hire the donor for one hour. An organization would prefer an unconstrained gift of w dollars to a constrained gift of the same size. Thus, an individual interested only in helping a charity provide goods and services would give money.[2]

The Role of Taxation

So far I have ignored the fact that earnings are taxed. Incorporating this fact complicates the choice between money and time donations and provides a limited rationale for volunteering. In the presence of an income tax, the opportunity cost of volunteering is only the person's net of tax wage, which can be written as $w(1 - t)$, where t is the marginal tax rate. This hour volunteered again has a value to the charity of w^*, which is less than w but may not be less than $w(1 - t)$.

The choice between forms of giving is now different for individuals who itemize on their tax returns than for those who do not. An itemizer would, as above, give only money. Since money contributions are tax deductible, he or she could contribute either w dollars or one hour at the same cost of $w(1 - t)$. Since the w dollars are more valuable to the organization, the itemizer would not volunteer.

However, if the donor is not an itemizer, there may be reason to volunteer. A donation of w dollars will now cost the donor w, rather than $w(1 - t)$, since the donation is not tax deductible. Therefore, for a cost of $w(1 - t)$, the donor can either volunteer one hour, worth w^* to the charity, or contribute $w(1 - t)$ dollars. If $w^* > w(1 - t)$, the donor will give time rather than money. However, most non-itemizers face low tax rates, so that it will pay for many of them to give money as well.[3]

There are two qualifications to this analysis. First, it is possible that individuals are more highly motivated in their role as volunteers than as paid workers. Thus, even if w represents an individual's greatest possible productivity in the wage labor market, it is possible that $w^* > w$, and it might "pay" for even an itemizer to volunteer.

Second, labor markets are imperfect so that individuals cannot always work as many hours for pay as they desire. Therefore, an individual's opportunity cost of time may be lower than his or her net wage and, again, it may pay to volunteer. On the other hand, someone who is forced to work longer hours than desired will have an opportunity cost of time that exceeds his or her wage.

Since the cost of volunteering is an individual's foregone wage, we would expect high wage earners to volunteer relatively infrequently—their time is simply too valuable. On the other hand, it is likely that high wage earners are particularly productive volunteers, so that there is an opposing tendency for them to volunteer more than low wage earners. What really matters, then, in determining volunteer hours, is the difference between one's value as paid labor and as a volunteer—the greater this difference the less likely one is to volunteer.

To summarize, this "collective output" model predicts that tax itemizers will never volunteer and that non-itemizers will give either money or time, depending on whether w^* is greater or less than $w(1 - t)$. If, in addition, the productivity of a volunteer, w^*, remains constant as he or she donates more hours, then we can further conclude that no individual will give both money and time to the same charity—each will simply choose the cheapest way of financing the charitable output.

Money, Time, and Government Policy

One important but overlooked issue for policy toward the charitable sector is the relationship between donations of money and time. The Tax Reform Act of 1986, for instance, will reduce contributions of cash in the future, since it raises the price of giving for most donors. (I examine the tax reform in detail in Chapter 9.) If donors respond to the tax law changes by simply switching from giving money to volunteering time, there may be little impact on the ability of charities to provide goods and services. On the other hand, if giving of both types falls off, the effect of tax reform on the nonprofit sector will be especially harsh.

The issue, in economic terms, is whether donations of money and time are substitutes or complements. In the "collective goods" model, the answer is clear—the two forms of giving are not just substitutes, but perfect substitutes. Donors simply choose the form of giving that provides the cheapest means of financing charitable goods and services. Therefore, any policy that increases the price of one form of giving—such as the Tax Reform Act of 1986—will induce a switch into giving in the other form, with little effect on the total resources of the nonprofit sector.

This perfect substitutability also implies that the two forms of giving will respond to government policies in similar fashions. If, for instance, cuts in government spending increase the demand for charitable output by donors, contributions of both money and time will rise. The analysis in Chapters 2 through 4 would apply to volunteering as well as money donations.

A "PRIVATE GOODS" MODEL OF VOLUNTEERING

The preceding model of volunteering has a number of strong, and unrealistic, implications. Many individuals do give both money and time. In fact, volunteers are more likely than nonvolunteers to give money.[4] In addition, many itemizers do volunteer. Both of these facts are ruled out by the "collective goods" model of volunteering.

Volunteers may be concerned with more than simply increasing the collective output of charitable organizations. They may, for instance, enjoy the interaction with other volunteers, or with the clients served by the charity. A donor may also enjoy the prestige or good name in the community that volunteering often brings. Finally, an individual may simply enjoy knowing that he or she has performed a good deed. All of these "goods" are essentially private, rather than collective, in nature.

Of course, money donors may also receive private benefit. However, if donors are motivated by certain private goals, it may pay to volunteer even if money donations are a less costly method of financing charitable output. If, for instance, it is easier to "buy" a good name in the community by volunteering than by donating money because volunteering is a more visible act, or if associations formed while volunteering are of value, people may give time even if the managers of charitable organizations would prefer that they give money.

Implications of a Private Motive for Giving

To the extent that time and money are donated for different reasons, they will be less close substitutes for a donor. Thus, a donor may well give both money and time as the least costly way of both financing charitable output and acquiring the private benefit. Also, a change in the price of one form of giving need not lead to a large shift into giving of the other type as it did in the collective goods model, although as long as some overlap exists in the reasons for giving money and time, we might expect some such shift.

The analysis of the impact of government spending changes is also different with a private motive. Again, this can be seen as a matter of the extent to which the goods purchased by volunteering are close substitutes to another good—here, government output. In the extreme case in which time is donated only for private benefits—such as prestige or association with other volunteers or clients, for which government output is a poor substitute, cuts in government output will have little if any effect on volunteering. Similarly, a reduction in government support of the nonprofit sector will reduce the level of collective output but have little or no impact on demand for the private goods provided by volunteering. To the extent, then, that private motives are more important in explaining volunteering than money donations, donations of time will be less responsive to government spending policies than are contributions of cash.

Finally, the more important is the private motive relative to the collective one, the less of a factor free riding is in explaining volunteering. In fact, increased volunteering by others may induce additional volunteering by an individual, due to the demonstration effects noted in Chapter 2. In general, the existence of private motives for giving make the behavior of a donor less dependent on the actions both of government and other donors.

VOLUNTEERING AND INFLUENCE

Introducing a private benefit to volunteering provides one way to differentiate giving of time from donations of money and, therefore, provides a rationale for volunteering. There are, however, other important differences between giving money and time. In particular, volunteers can often exert influence over the actions of a charity more easily than can a money donor. I turn now to examine more closely this influence motive.

A consumer can benefit from either an increase in the output of a charity that he or she values or from a movement in output type, q, toward his or her preferred value. For instance, each consumer has some demand (possibly zero) for day care services from a particular center that depends, in part, on the type of care provided by the center. Different centers may, for example, follow different educational philosophies or have different religious orientations. A consumer valuing day care services as a collective good will gain either if the output of a center increases—as measured, say, by students enrolled—or if the philosophy of the center moves closer to his or her own.

Suppose for simplicity that volunteers, but not money donors, can influence q. Money donations, then, "buy" increased output only, while volunteering can buy influence as well as output. In reality, donations of money—particularly large ones—can purchase influence as well. However, it seems likely that influence is more easily obtained by volunteering than by donating money, particularly for donors with limited financial resources. A donor's choice between giving money and time, then, may be viewed as a choice between the least costly method of financing charitable output—money donations—and a more costly method of financing the output—volunteering—which also provides the opportunity for influence.

The gain to a donor from volunteering rather than giving money depends, therefore, on the extent to which he or she can exert influence, and this ability to exert influence depends, in turn, on the characteristics both of the individuals volunteering and the organizations to which they give. A new organization, for example, may have a less well-defined philosophy, or may have a power structure that is more easily penetrated than an older, more established one. Therefore, we would expect to see a move from reliance on volunteers to greater professionalization and heavier reliance on money donations, as a charity ages. In addition, since the ability to exert influence varies from charity to charity, it would not be surprising to see an individual volunteering for one organization while giving money to another.

It is also likely that a donor will find it easier to influence an organization when its ideology is already fairly close to his or her own. On the other hand, if a charity's ideology is already identical, or nearly so, to a donor's, there may be little reason for the donor to attempt to exert influence, and he or she may simply give money. In effect, the individual will free ride on the influence of volunteers with preferences similar to his or her own. Output type, like the output itself, has a collective aspect.

Characteristics of the donor will also make volunteering as a means to gain influence more or less attractive. Those with supervisory or management skills will be in a particularly good position to influence an organization's decisions, as may those with more years of formal schooling.

Finally, the desire to volunteer will depend on the value that an individual places on influence. A donor may be able to exert influence but have little interest in doing so. Volunteering will tend to attract those for whom output type, or ideology, is particularly important, while money donors may be more concerned with simply increasing charitable output in general, without having any strong convictions about the kinds of goods and services that should be provided.

Money and Time as Potential Complements

If this "influence" model explains a significant portion of volunteering, then our expectation that money and time donations are substitutes may have to be reconsidered. Suppose that the cost of volunteering rises because tax rates on earnings are reduced—as in the Tax Reform Act of 1986. Consumers now find it more costly than before to exert influence over charitable organizations and, so, volunteer less. It is quite plausible that these individuals, seeing their influence diminished, may reduce their gifts of money as well. Money and time donations, then, may be complements. Looking ahead, our empirical analysis indicates such a complementary relationship, suggesting that the influence model has explanatory power.

Government Policies, Influence, and Volunteering

Government policies may influence volunteering either by making it more or less costly or effective in providing influence, or by making influence less valuable to the donor.

We know that a tax rate cut tends to reduce hours donated by making volunteering more costly. The story is somewhat more complex than this, however, since tax law changes also affect the cost of giving money and this, in turn, influences volunteer behavior. The 1986 tax reform, for instance, increases the cost of giving money and this may either induce a switch into volunteering—offsetting, in part, the direct effect on the cost of giving time—or lead to a further fall in hours donated. As will be discussed in Chapter 9, the latter seems more likely.

Government spending and regulatory policies also can affect volunteering-as-influence. Suppose, for instance, that a cut in government spending induces an increased demand for charitable output. While this will cause contributions of money to increase, the direction of the effect on volunteering is uncertain. On one hand, the increased demand for output could lead individuals to desire more influence as well, and so to volunteer more. However, it could also cause donors to focus more on the quantity of services provided and less on the type, and so to reduce contributions of time.

Government support of the charitable sector, with its accompanying constraints, would likely reduce volunteering by limiting an organization's ability to choose q, and so the potential scope of volunteer influence. An organization that receives most of its revenue from government to carry out a specific program will not be in a position to respond to pressure from volunteers to change their activities.

Charities that successfully pursue government grants, then, may see the nature of their organizations change, from those with heavy reliance on volunteers to those that depend on grants and contributions of cash to hire professional staff. Thus, nonprofit sector leaders have expressed concern that the increased reliance of charitable organizations on government as a source of revenue may have greatly diminished the voluntary nature of nonprofit sector activities and led to increased bureaucratization.

IMPERFECT INFORMATION AND THE SEARCH MODEL OF VOLUNTEERING

Donors are often uncertain about the quality of an organization, either in terms of the type of output provided or the efficiency with which it is produced. Volunteering provides an opportunity to learn about the quality of charities, and this acquisition of information provides yet another reason for giving time. In addition, even if the desire for information does not motivate volunteering, giving time may nevertheless generate information as a side benefit, and this new information will influence the donor's future behavior.

Suppose that money and time play distinct roles for donors—gifts of money contribute to the production of output only, while volunteering provides information about output quality but does not produce output. This is clearly unrealistic; however, it serves as a useful starting point. As in previous chapters, quality depends on output type and efficiency. Each potential donor is uncertain about output quality and so must decide how much, if any, information to gather about each charity to which he or she is contemplating giving. The additional information is of value to the donor only because it allows better decisions to be made regarding charitable gifts. The information is assumed to have no value per se, apart from its influence on subsequent behavior.

Each consumer, even before volunteering, has beliefs about the quality of each organization of which he or she is aware. These beliefs can be expressed in terms of expected quality—measured by efficiency and output type—which represents the person's best guess, and a variance about the expectation, reflecting the level of certainty with which the belief is held. The greater the variance, the less confident is the donor about his or her best guess. These prior beliefs are formed with information from many sources—solicitations, the news media, comments from friends, or perhaps simply casual observation, or prejudices. If no additional information could be obtained, a donor would be forced to make decisions based on the imperfect prior information. However, by choosing the number of hours to volunteer a donor can, in effect, choose the desired amount of information to gather.

Volunteering can be viewed as constituting a search across charitable organizations.[5] The new information acquired by volunteering will move the donor's expectation of quality closer to that observed during volunteering and will reduce the variance around that expectation. More information is always better than less, but gathering that information is not free. Donors will volunteer to the point at which the marginal benefit—in terms of the value of improved gift giving—just equals the marginal cost of time foregone. Since the marginal value of information generated by each successive hour of volunteering likely declines, while the cost does not, donors will typically stop short of acquiring perfect information.

In general, it is difficult to say much about how the demand for information, and so the extent of volunteering, will be affected by changes in variables of interest to us here. However, if we restrict the volunteer's utility function to be of the Constant Elasticity of Substitution (C.E.S.) family we can reach a number of conclusions.[6] If volunteering is motivated solely by the demand for information:

1. As the cost of acquiring information by volunteering increases, hours volunteered fall.
2. The demand for information, and so volunteering, increases with income.
3. People volunteer more for organizations about which they have little prior information than for charities about which they know a great deal.
4. Individuals volunteer less for organizations which they believe are of either very high or very low quality than for those they believe are of moderate quality.
5. People volunteer less for organizations that produce goods on which they place either very high or very low values.
6. Demand for information about goods whose purchase prices are very low or very high will be low. So, as the price of a contribution of money rises, hours volunteered will first rise, then fall. Whether money and time donations are substitutes or complements depends on the range of prices of money donations considered.

The intuition behind the first two results seems clear; the other conclusions merit discussion. It is crucial to keep in mind that information has value here only if it alters a donor's subsequent behavior. If volunteering simply confirms a donor's prior beliefs, then it has no impact on the donor's behavior, and the volunteering has generated no benefit, only costs. The less information one has about an organization, the more likely it is that any new information will alter one's donative behavior, and so the more likely the information will be of value. If an individual has perfect information about a charity's activities, then volunteering can, in this model, provide no benefits (result 3).

The remaining results have similar explanations. If, for instance, I expect that an organization is of very low quality, it is unlikely that any information I obtain will cause me to switch from planning not to give to deciding to give. By the same token, if I expect the organization to be of extremely high quality, information gained by volunteering is unlikely to dissuade me from giving. Thus, in either case, volunteering is unlikely to generate large benefits.

While these results have some intuitive appeal, they do not all seem to coincide well with casual observation or introspection.

People seem to often volunteer for organizations about which they know quite a bit or have extremely strong opinions. This would seem to indicate that the search for information provides, at best, a partial explanation of volunteering. I return to consider modifications in the model, below. First, however, I trace the implications for government policy of this "pure" search model.

Government, Search, and Volunteering

Government tax and spending policies can influence volunteering-as-search in a variety of ways. First, tax policy can affect the opportunity cost of volunteering. Second, any policy change that affects the demand for charitable output—such as a cut in government spending—also affects demand for information about the quality of charities, although in a complex fashion. Finally, and probably most important, government support of charities provides information about the quality of organizations and so reduces the value of volunteering to the donor.

Suppose that a cut in government spending increases demand for charitable goods and services. How will this affect volunteering-as-search? Recall that the demand for information about a charity, and so the desire to volunteer, is low when demand for the output of that charity is either very low or very high. Cuts in government spending to a sufficiently low level will make the demand for charitable output so strong that the demand for information and thus volunteering is reduced, even while contributions of money are rising.

At higher levels of government spending, however, budget cuts will increase demand for charity from very low to moderate levels and so increase donors' need to know about organization quality. Both money donations and volunteering would rise. Thus, according to this search model, volunteering should have an inverted U-shaped relationship with government output, first rising as government increases its output, then falling.

Finally, as discussed in Chapter 4, government support provides information about the quality of organizations. To simplify, suppose that when government supports a charity, it fixes its q at some value, q^*, which it then announces to the public. Donors, now certain about the quality of the supported organization, will no longer volunteer, although they may have additional incentive to give money. More generally, if regulation increases donors' prior information, it reduces expected benefits from volunteering. This result is quite similar to that discussed above, regarding the impact of regulation on volunteering to gain influence—increased ties with government reduce the ability of organizations to attract volunteers.

Modifying the Search Model

The analysis of volunteering-as-search has been made under several restrictive assumptions in order to isolate the implications of one particular motive for giving time. In particular, I assumed that volunteers give time only to search for information, and that volunteering has no effect on the level of charitable output produced. Here, I drop those assumptions.

Suppose that volunteering does increase charitable output but by less than a donation of money that is equally costly to the donor. How would this modify the results from the "search only" model? First, while that model predicts that people will volunteer for organizations about which they know the least, this will likely not be the case when volunteering increases output as well. Donors will demand less output from organizations about which they know the least, offsetting, at least in part, the influence of the demand for information. It seems plausible that donors must acquire some minimum level of prior information about an organization before they give money or time. Beyond some threshold level of prior information, however, donors may well switch from volunteering to giving money, as the value of additional searching falls relative to the value of more output.

Other results would be similarly modified to reflect the twin goals of financing charitable output and gathering information. While those seeking only information would volunteer little for charities that produce goods for which they have very strong demands or for organizations they believe to be of extremely high quality, joint considerations of financing output and gathering information might dictate volunteering at these charities.

The preceding analysis is complicated if consumers are well informed about one dimension of quality—say, output type—while poorly informed about the other, efficiency. In this case, it may be optimal for a donor to volunteer only for a small number of organizations whose ideologies are known to be close to his or her preferred ideology in order to gather information about relative efficiency.

Finally, the analysis assumes that search is a motive for volunteering. However, whatever the initial reason for giving time, any information acquired while volunteering will affect donations of money. Increased certainty about quality, brought about by volunteering, will lead a risk-averse donor to want to give more money to an organization, other things being equal. Furthermore, if the additional information changes the donor's expectation of quality, that too will influence giving, apart from any increased degree of certainty.

The expected level of quality may be raised or lowered by the additional information—i.e., the volunteer may be happily surprised or disappointed by what he or she finds. If the information acquired by the volunteer makes him or her revise the expectation of quality upward, this reinforces the impact of the increased certainty, and donations of money to the charity should rise. However, even if the information is somewhat disappointing—causing a downward revision of the expected quality level—money contributions may still rise, as the increased certainty may more than offset any change in expectation.

We might expect, then, that whatever the motivation for volunteering, a decline in the cost of giving time will tend to increase contributions of money. That is, money and time donations will be complements. However, this result is not necessarily symmetric: a fall in the price of money donations need not affect the extent of volunteering, as giving money does not typically generate information for the donor.

VOLUNTEERING AS JOB TRAINING

Surveys as well as anecdotal evidence indicate that many volunteers are motivated by a desire to gain job skills, or "human capital" in order to increase future earnings.[7] Organizations hoping to attract volunteers will often stress this aspect of volunteering, and some even formalize it in their programs. For instance, VIGOR (Volunteers in Government), a volunteer program run by the City of New Orleans, offers volunteers city civil service credit necessary for some paid municipal employment. Their literature also informs potential volunteers that VIGOR is "happy to write recommendations to employers or be of any other assistance to volunteers."

The wage received by a worker in any job may be less than his or her total benefit from that job since employment may provide training or investment in human capital, that will increase future wages.[8] A worker will choose a job that pays a wage less than the maximum obtainable if the training component of the job is expected to allow an increase in future wages larger, in present value, than the foregone present wages. These foregone wages are, in effect, the price paid by the worker for training. For a volunteer, the wage rate received is zero, so the implicit price of training is the entire wage that the volunteer could have received in a paying job, if that job provided no training.[9]

Suppose a worker is confronted with just two choices—a paying job that offers a wage of w but no training, and a volunteer job that includes the opportunity to obtain job skills but provides no other benefits. The volunteer job will be chosen if the present value of future returns from the skills acquired exceeds the net-of-tax wages foregone by volunteering.[10]

This model predicts that the likelihood of volunteering increases as the current wage rate falls, the tax rate on earnings rises, and the age of the individual falls. The intuition behind these results is clear. The lower the wage rate foregone, the more attractive is volunteering. Similarly, the higher the tax rate on those earnings, the less take-home pay the volunteer foregoes and the less costly is the training acquired by volunteering. Finally, younger donors have more years over which to capitalize on gains from training and, so, greater incentive to volunteer.

The rate at which skills can be learned and used to increase future wages will also influence volunteering, and this rate will depend on the characteristics of the volunteer. Rosen (1972) suggests that formal schooling increases the ability of an individual to take advantage of job training. We would expect, then, that more highly educated individuals will volunteer more often. So, the most likely volunteer—if job training is the motivation for giving time—would be a highly educated young person with the opportunity to earn only a relatively low wage, e.g., a recent liberal arts graduate or a college-educated woman who has been out of the job market for several years.

Volunteers and the Labor Market

In previous analyses of on-the-job training, in which the role of volunteering has been ignored, it has been noted that the minimum wage law may act to reduce on-the-job training. If an individual could earn only the minimum wage or less in a free labor market, he or she would be unable to "purchase" any training by voluntarily taking a cut in pay, since a reduction in wages would put that individual's wage below the legal limit. This has led some (e.g., Rosen, 1972) to suggest that the minimum wage should be lower for younger workers—who would demand more on-the-job training if they could—than for older workers.

However, volunteer labor is, in effect, an exception to the minimum wage law. So, those persons whose market wage, in the absence of on-the-job training, would be at or below the minimum wage can acquire job skills by volunteering (or through job-training programs unrelated to their job). Those with market wages far above the minimum wage, however, may gain such training by accepting implicit reductions in wages. This gives an additional reason—besides the opportunity cost of time—to expect low-wage individuals to volunteer more than those with high earnings.

Job Training and Contributions of Money

If time is volunteered solely to acquire job skills while money is donated in order to increase charitable output, there is no reason to expect time and money donations to be close substitutes. The two forms of giving could be complements if the amount of job training received by a volunteer depends on the amount of money he or she contributes; for instance, money donors may be given the choice of jobs with a large training component. That is, the price of the training received may be greater than the wages foregone—the volunteer may be required to give some money as well.

Government Policies and Volunteering as Investment

If job training is the motivation for giving time, then there would seem to be little role for government spending policies to play in affecting volunteering. Increased regulation of the charitable sector may influence volunteering somewhat if the value of training received by volunteers depends on the type of output produced by the charity. Skills acquired by volunteers may be specific to particular industries or firms, and regulated firms that produce different types of goods and services may provide training that is more or less valuable in terms of future earnings. It is difficult, however, to predict the general direction of this effect.

This is the same general conclusion reached in the above "private goods" model. In fact, this training model is a special case of the private goods model, with the private good being increased future earnings. In this special case, however, additional predictions regarding the impact of individual characteristics—such as age and education—are possible.

THE SUPPLY OF VOLUNTEER TIME: SUMMARY

Each of the models of volunteering discussed in this chapter has different implications, particularly for the likely effect of government policies on volunteering and for the relationship between money and time donations.

Government Policies

A decrease in tax rates has a similar effect in all models; by raising the opportunity cost of volunteering, a tax cut will increase hours donated regardless of the motivation for giving time.

Increased government spending on production of output will tend to decrease hours volunteered in the "collective output" model, as it does in the case of money donations. The search model predicts that hours donated will first rise and then fall with increases in government output, and the "influence" model provides ambiguous predictions. Given that volunteers almost certainly have mixed motives, it is likely that hours donated respond less elastically to changes in government output than do contributions of cash.

Both the influence and search models predict that constraints associated with government support reduce hours volunteered. Thus, in a mixed motives explanation of volunteering, regulation should have a more negative impact on volunteering than on money contributions. Increased regulation will affect both the level and mix—between money and time—of donations.

Money and Time

Contributions of money and time may be substitutes, complements, or unrelated, depending on the reason or reasons that people give each. The collective goods model of volunteering assumes that money and time are donated for the same reason; thus they are perfect substitutes. The other models are less clear in their predictions. If influence provides an important reason for volunteering, then money and time donations may be complements, since the closer a charity's output type is to an individual's preferred type, the more output he or she will demand from that organization. If time donated provides information about firm quality, there may also be reason to expect that increased volunteering will encourage increased money donations.

While the analysis makes no strong prediction about the relationship of money and time in general, it does imply that certain types of volunteer jobs—such as leadership roles—that involve greater influence will be more complementary with money donations than other types of volunteer activities—such as manual labor—which provide little opportunity to exert influence. The empirical analysis in Chapter 7 deals separately with various types of volunteer activities.

THE DEMAND FOR VOLUNTEERS

To this point, I have examined the supply of volunteer labor but have not discussed the demand of charities for volunteers. Organizations have been viewed as passive, simply accepting all volunteers who happen their way.

In fact, attracting and utilizing volunteers is costly to a charity. Solicitations may be necessary to attract volunteers, as in the case of money donors, but, in addition, training and supervising volunteers diverts resources from other uses. Charitable organizations, then, must choose an optimal amount to spend on recruiting and employing volunteers and so, implicitly, an optimal number of volunteers.

In Chapter 4, I examined the process by which charities determine their optimal level of expenditures to solicit money donations. If volunteers are motivated primarily by their desire to expand collective charitable output, that analysis is applicable here as well. Charities provide information to potential money and time donors, soliciting the most promising donors first. As argued in Chapter 4, the optimal level of spending on solicitations occurs when the last dollar so spent raises just one dollar's worth of giving; here, giving of both money and time. The organization must determine how valuable it considers volunteer labor in order to make this calculation.

To the extent that volunteering can be viewed as a search for information, soliciting may be less effective at attracting volunteers than money donors. By providing information about the organization, a solicitation may increase demand for the output of that organization, and thus money donations, while reducing the need to volunteer to gain information.

The training and supervising of volunteers is likely to involve substantial setup costs—e.g., hiring a director of volunteers— with the marginal cost falling as additional volunteers are employed. Thus, there may be a tendency for organizations to either use no volunteers or to have a substantial program. Organizations may, and often do, turn down volunteer labor, since it is unpaid, but not free.

NOTES

1. If a volunteer does not work in the wage labor market, w will represent the value of time spent in home production.

2. As noted in Chapter 4, donors may sometimes want to constrain the recipient organization by volunteering rather than giving money.

3. Long (1977) notes that making money donations tax deductible, but not the value of volunteer hours donated, maintains neutrality be-

tween forms of giving since the cost of a gift of time is already the net-of-tax wage rate.

4. A 1986 survey by Yankelovich, Skelly, and White, Inc., *The Charitable Behavior of Americans*, indicates that in 1984 individuals who volunteered some time gave an average of 2.8 percent of their income as money donations, compared with 2.0 percent for nonvolunteers.

5. For a discussion of search in other economic contexts see, e.g., Hey (1979).

6. See Kihlstrom (1974).

7. For instance, in a survey conducted by the Gallup Organization, *Americans Volunteer*, October 1985, 10 percent of the respondents cited "wanted to learn and get the experience" as a reason for volunteering, and 36 percent cited "had an interest in the work or activity." Either of these can be interpreted as involving job training. It is not important for this analysis whether volunteering provides a tangible skill or merely serves as a signaling device to potential employers. All that is necessary is that volunteering increases future wages.

8. See Rosen (1972) for a discussion of the role of investment in human capital on a worker's job choice.

9. If there are other benefits from volunteering, such as the acquisition of influence or information, then the cost of the training received is less than the foregone wage.

10. The value of future returns, V, from a unit of human capital can be written (see Rosen, 1972) as:

$$V = R/r \, (1 - e^{-r(N - n)})$$

where n is the age of the worker, N is the total number of years over which returns will be realized, R is the rate of return on a unit of human capital, and r is the discount rate. Thus, the present value of training is V times the increase in human capital, k. Volunteering will be chosen if and only if:

$$kR/r \, (1 - e^{-r(N - n)}) > w(1 - t)$$

where w is the wage rate in the paying job and t is the marginal tax rate.

6.

Contributions of Money:
Empirical Evidence

INTRODUCTION

The preceding chapters have presented a theory of charitable
giving of money and time. Each of the models presented make
predictions, particularly regarding the impact of various government policies on donations and the relationship between contributions of money and time. This and the following chapter test
some of those predictions. Here I focus on donations of money;
Chapter 7 examines volunteering. The results presented allow an
evaluation of the relevance of the models discussed and permit
the estimation of the quantitative effects of various policy changes
on giving.

I begin by briefly reviewing the implications of the preceding
analysis of money donations. This will set the stage for the empirical estimation of a money donations equation.

Theoretical Implications

The preceding analysis indicates that an individual's contributions of money depend broadly on his or her demand for charitable goods and services and the relative costs of providing that

output via money and time donations. The demand for charity will, in turn, depend on the usual economic factors, such as the prices of charity and other goods as well as income. In addition, however, it will depend on a number of factors unique to collective goods.

First, the demand for charitable output, and thus donations, will depend on the level of government production of goods that are either substitutes for, or complements of, charity. Government support of charities also influences the types of goods and services provided by these organizations, and so affects giving. In addition, because donors often have less than perfect information about the quality of charitable organizations, giving will depend on the extent to which information is supplied, for instance by government grants. Finally, charitable giving will be influenced by the amount given by other donors. The free-rider hypothesis predicts that as others increase their giving, any single donor will contribute less.

I turn now to the empirical analysis. First, I describe the data employed and discuss expected results based on the theoretical analysis above. Following that, I briefly describe the methodology employed, present the results, and discuss their implications.

DATA AND EXPECTED RESULTS

The Data Source

The principal data source for this analysis is the *National Survey of Philanthropy* (1974). This survey of 2,802 households provides detailed information about each household's charitable contributions of money and time: how much they gave (in 1973), to what sort of organizations they gave and, in the case of volunteering, what sort of jobs they performed. Information is also provided on household income, wealth, attitudes, and demographic characteristics. The state and county of residence is also known for a subset of the respondents, allowing a match of households with government spending data and data on state characteristics.[1]

While this survey is nearly fifteen years old, it remains the best data source with which to carry out the type of analysis done here. Far more information is available than from the tax return data typically used to study charitable giving. First, information on volunteering allows me to estimate equations for donations of both money and time. The inclusion of volunteering is crucial both because of its quantitative significance and because the relationship between gifts of money and time is of interest.

In addition, the breadth and depth of information available from the survey far exceeds that of any other available data source. For instance, attitudinal questions allow me to separate out, to some extent, the influence of preferences from those of economic variables, such as prices and income. More important, from the point of view of this book, is that knowing the zip code of respondents allows me to match each individual's data with the relevant information from his or her state and locality. Given the focus here on the role of government spending, such information is crucial.

Finally, unlike other data sources, the survey disaggregates giving of money and time by type of organization receiving the gift and breaks down volunteering by type of activity performed by the volunteer. The breakdown by organization type allows me to match giving data with government spending in the same field, such as social welfare or education. Previous analyses of the relationship between giving and government spending were able to examine only aggregate measures of each. As discussed below, this obscures some important effects. The breakdown of volunteering by type of activity allows a more thorough examination of the various models of volunteering presented in Chapter 5. Results suggest that using more aggregated data would overlook important phenomena.

For all these reasons, the *National Survey of Philanthropy* is the best data source for our purposes. The data source does, however, have its own shortcomings, which I discuss where applicable. Its primary, at least potential, shortcoming is its age. Note, however, that while the aggregate values of charitable giving, income, and government spending have all changed since 1974, there is no strong reason to believe that the relationship between these variables has been dramatically altered. Since it is these relationships, rather than any estimates of total giving, that interested me here, the age of the data need not be a severe problem. Needless to say, however, newer data would be preferable if they existed in the required detail. In Chapter 8, I supplement the survey data analysis with time series data from 1930 through 1986. The results of the analysis suggest that estimates using data from the 1960s and 1970s do a good job of predicting giving in the 1980s. This should make us feel more comfortable in applying the survey results to giving today.

The Dependent Variables

The first variable to be explained in this analysis is the number of dollars each household reported giving to all charitable organizations in 1973. Equations are also estimated in which the dependent variables are household donations of money to various types of charities:

1. health and medical
2. higher education
3. elementary education
4. social welfare
5. combined appeals (such as United Way)[2]

Explanatory Variables

I hypothesize that donations of money depend on the prices of providing charity via money and time donations, donor income, government spending, and giving by other donors. In addition, a number of other characteristics of the household and the state in which donors live are included as control variables.

Prices and Income

The cost of a money donation is measured by PRICE, which equals $(1 - t)$ for itemizers and 1 for non-itemizers, where t is the marginal tax rate in the absence of contributions.[3] The higher PRICE is the less, other things being equal, a donor will give.

The cost of giving time is proxied by an individual's net-of-tax wage (NETWAGE) since, if individuals are unconstrained in their uses of time, they will equate the value of their time across all activities. If, however, people are constrained to work more or less than their desired number of hours, then the net wage will not equal the opportunity cost of time. In that case, other factors—such as the number of children in the household—may affect the cost of volunteering. (I discuss such factors below.) A positive coefficient for NETWAGE indicates that money and time are substitutes, while a negative coefficient implies they are complements.

NETWAGE is not directly observed in the sample. Rather, it is constructed from data on earnings and hours worked.[4] Such a construction, however, is possible only for single-earner households, so that the sample is limited to such households.[5]

The concept of income used here is full or potential income, defined as an individual's income if he or she worked year round and full time (2,000 hours per year). The measure, INCOME, is preferable to actual income, since actual hours worked are determined simultaneously with hours volunteered. People who volunteer many hours will tend to work fewer hours for pay and thus have lower incomes than those who do not volunteer much time. I expect the coefficient for income to be positive.

Government Expenditures

The analysis of Chapters 2 through 4 indicates that government output and support of the charitable sector will each affect donations of money. Government spending data, however, include spending on both government production and grants to (and purchases of service from) charities. I attempt to at least partially disentangle the impact of the two types of spending on giving by comparing the impact of changes in some categories of government spending—such as cash transfers to the needy—that do not include grants to the charitable sector, with those types—such as spending on social services—that do include such grants.[6]

In the aggregate money donations equation, the government spending variables included are per capita total state and local government expenditures for 1973 in the respondent's state and locality—STATEGOV and LOCGOV. In the disaggregated equations, the categories of state and local government expenditures included are those that seem most closely related to the type of charity being examined. The categories of state spending are cash transfers to the needy (CASH), other welfare spending (WELFARE), spending on higher education (HIED), lower educations (LOWED), hospitals (HOSP) and other health (HEALTH). Local government spending is disaggregated only into spending on social welfare (LOCSW).[7]

An increase in government output will decrease giving if governmental and charitable output are substitutes and increase donations if they are complements. The coefficient for CASH—which does not include grants to charity—will capture only this "substitution effect." Coefficients for other government spending variables, however, will reflect both this effect and the impact of any change in government support of the charitable sector. This support can, as discussed, influence giving in a number of ways. First, any increase in charitable output brought about by government grants will tend to crowd out donations. In addition, grants are generally accompanied by constraints on the type of goods and services provided and may also influence the efficiency of an organization. Finally, a grant may provide information about a charity, which would encourage giving. The coefficients for these other spending variables will tell us something about the relative importance of these various effects.

Free-Rider Behavior

As giving by others increases, a donor may choose to reduce his or her own giving by free riding. Alternatively, "demonstration effects" may cause donors to give more as those around them increase contributions. I proxy giving by others with the variable OTHGIV, per capita contributions claimed as deductions on personal income tax by taxpayers in the donor's home state in 1973. This is obviously a very rough measure of the concept we seek. In particular, the relevant group of "others" for any donor may be much narrower than all state residents.

Two other sets of variables are included to capture free-rider effects. The first is community size. Olson (1968) and Buchanan

(1965) argue that free riding increases with group size. Thus, residents of large cities may give less than those of small towns. Community size is represented by dummy variables for residents of large cities (LCITY), medium-sized cities (MCITY), small cities (SCITY) or suburbs (SUBCITY). The excluded group is residents of rural areas. If free riding is important, we would expect the coefficients to be negative for each of the included variables.

In addition, I include the number of years the household has lived in its neighborhood (YRNBH).[8] I expect that the longer a potential donor lives in a community, the easier his or her actions—such as whether he or she donates—can be learned, and the more important the attitudes of neighbors become. Thus, free riding will become more difficult as YRNBH increases.

State Socioeconomic Variables

To the extent that charitable giving implies income redistribution to the poor,[9] we would expect giving to vary with the need for such redistribution. I include per capita income in the respondent's home state (PCINC) and percent in his or her home county below the poverty line (PERPOOR).

Household Characteristics

A number of demographic characteristics of the household that may affect demand for charity are included as well. I control for the age (AGE), sex (FEMALE = 1 if female, 0 male), marital status (MARRIED = 1 if married, 0 otherwise), race (WHITE = 1 if white, 0 otherwise) and level of educational attainment (EDUC).[10]

In addition, the presence of children is captured by YGKID = 1 if child under 5 in household, 0 otherwise; and OTHKID = 1 if child between 5 and 17 in household, 0 otherwise. A household with more children will demand more of certain charitable goods, such as education or recreation.[11] In addition, the presence of children may increase one's opportunity cost of time, increasing money donations if money and time are substitutes and decreasing contributions of money if the two are complements.

Donor Attitudes

Finally, I include a set of variables to account for differences in donor backgrounds and attitudes toward philanthropy: BACKED = 1 if father completed high school, 0 otherwise; BACKREL = 1 if parents attended religious services at least once per week, 0 otherwise; and BACKGIVE = 1 if parents gave regularly to charity, 0 otherwise. In addition, I include HELPER, the number of hours spent by the respondent, per year, helping friends, neighbors and relatives outside the household.

RESULTS AND IMPLICATIONS

Many respondents to the survey gave no money or time to charity.[12] Ordinary least squares regression analysis will, therefore, produce biased coefficient estimates. Given this feature of the data, Tobin's procedure for limited dependent variables (Tobit) is a reasonable approach to estimation.[13]

Price and Income Elasticities[14]

Table 6.1 shows the estimated price and income elasticities for aggregate money contributions as well as for contributions to particular types of charity.[15] The first conclusion that can be reached is that money contributions are quite responsive to changes in price. The price elasticity for aggregate giving, −2.79, is a good deal larger (in absolute value) than previous studies which, as shown in Table 6.2, have mainly varied between 1 and 1.5.[16]

Differences in results may come from several sources. First, the data source employed here is different from all the other studies noted, with the exception of Boskin and Feldstein (1977). That study, which focused on low-income donors, also estimated a price elasticity significantly higher than the consensus. The survey data has an advantage over the tax data employed in most other studies in that it includes both itemizers and non-itemizers.

In addition, my equations contain a large number of control

Table 6.1
Estimated Price and Income Elasticities for Money Donations

Type of Charity	Elasticities		
	Price	Income	Cross-Price
Aggregate	-2.79**	0.76**	-0.86**
Welfare	-4.97	0.43	-2.68*
Higher Education	-2.77	0.21	-0.23
Lower Education	-8.77**	-0.11	0.09
Health	-4.82**	0.55	-0.74*
Combined Appeal	-3.19**	0.93**	-1.32**

*Coefficient significant at .10 or better.

**Coefficients significant at .01 or better.

variables that are omitted from other studies. These studies typically regress contributions on price and income and a small number of other variables available from tax returns, such as age and marital status. In particular, other studies have been unable to control for differences in background and attitudes.

A price elasticity greater than 1 (in absolute value) indicates that the tax deductibility of donations stimulates more in contributions than it costs in terms of foregone tax revenue.[17] Thus, deductibility represents a less costly, or more efficient, means for the government to support charities than direct grants.

There are, however, a number of other issues involved in evaluating the desirability of allowing charitable donations to be tax deductible. First, it has been argued[18] that a tax credit is fairer than deductibility, since a credit offers the same subsidy per dollar donated for all taxpayers, while a deduction, in effect, provides larger subsidies for higher income taxpayers, who face a higher tax rate.

In addition, while deductibility may be more efficient than direct government expenditures, the mix of activities supported by each are quite different. Replacing direct government spending with deductibility of contributions allows individuals-as-donors

Table 6.2
Estimated Price and Income Elasticities from Previous Studies

Study	Elasticities	
	Price	Income
Taussig (1967)	-0.10	1.33
Schwartz (1970)[a]	-0.79	0.76
Feldstein (1975a)	-1.26	0.20
Feldstein and Taylor (1976)	-1.42	0.77
Feldstein and Clotfelter (1976)	-1.55	0.80
Boskin and Feldstein (1977)[b]	-2.54	0.69
Reece (1979)	-1.40	0.55
Clotfelter (1980)	-1.41	0.53
Reece and Zeischang (1985)	-0.85	1.43

[a]For individuals with adjusted gross income between $10,000 and $100,000 only. [b]For individuals with income between $1,000 and $10,000 only.

to exercise more power relative to individuals-as-voters, and this may be undesirable.

The negative cross-price elasticities[19] indicate that donations of money and time are complements. Therefore, any policy change that discourages volunteering—such as a reduction in tax rates on earnings—would reduce contributions of money as well as time. This result is consistent with both the search and influence models of volunteering but not with the simple collective goods model. I discuss this issue further when I examine separate volunteer activities.

The estimated income elasticities are generally positive, as expected, and similar to those of previous studies. The results indicate that the wealthy, other things being equal, give more than the poor, but that they give a smaller proportion of their income. This aggregate result, however, masks a huge degree of variance

Table 6.3
Elasticity of Money Donations with Respect to Per Capita Government Expenditures

Type of Expenditure	Type of Charity[a]	
	Aggregate	Welfare
STATEGOV	+1.89**	
LOCGOV	-1.13**	
CASH		-2.88**
WELFARE		4.56**
LOCSW		0.47

[a]Results for other types of charity are presented in Appendix B to this chapter.

**Coefficient significant at .01 or better.

in giving by the wealthy. Auten and Rudney (1988), for instance, report that the most generous 5 percent of individuals earning more than one million dollars per year account for 80 percent of giving by that group.

Government Spending and Charitable Giving

The impact of government spending on charitable donations of money is a primary focus of this analysis. The results indicate that government spending exerts a powerful influence on giving. In addition, the impact of government spending on giving depends, as expected, on the extent to which such spending includes grants to charity.

Aggregate donations of money rise as local governments cut their budgets but fall as state spending is decreased (Table 6.3). The elasticities imply that one dollar fall in local spending leads to a 66 cent rise in giving, while a dollar cut in state spending brings about a further 34 cent fall in donations.[20] An interpretation of this result is that charity is a substitute for local government output, but a complement of state output. However, the result may also be due to differences in the extent to which state and local governments provide services via support of the charitable sector. Government-imposed constraints on output type and the seal of approval implicit in government support could, as discussed, encourage additional charitable giving.[21]

When we look at contributions to social welfare charities we again see mixed results. Donations of money rise as cash transfers are cut but fall as other welfare spending decreases. This result is, however, more easily interpreted than that for aggregate giving. Since CASH goes directly to the needy and is not funneled through the charitable sector, a fall in CASH has no direct effect on government support to the charitable sector. However, a great deal of noncash social services are provided via the charitable sector.[22]

It appears that cuts in government support for the charitable sector lead to decreases in charitable giving. Rather than compensating for government spending reductions, the response of donors appears to exacerbate the impact on the provision of social services. Donors do appear, however, to respond to cuts in cash transfers to the needy by increasing their own giving. The results indicate that a dollar reduction in per capita cash transfers would lead to a six cent rise in per capita giving to welfare. However, a one dollar cut in other welfare expenditures would bring about an additional fall of five cents.[23]

Thus, whether government spending crowds out charitable giving depends on precisely what sorts of government spending and charitable giving are examined. This suggests that the mix of government spending could be manipulated to encourage donations. A one dollar cut in both CASH and WELFARE, for instance, would offset each other, and the overall impact on giving would be very small. However, replacing a dollar of cash transfers with a dollar of other welfare spending would lead to a significant rise in money donations of 11 cents.

Previous analyses[24] of crowding out have used more aggregated government spending data, such as measures of total social welfare spending, which obscure the differences noted here. In addition, those studies attempt to explain aggregate giving rather than giving to particular types of charity. However, there

Table 6.4
Evidence on Free-Rider Behavior: Coefficients on OTHGIV and YRNBH

Type of Charity	OTHGIV	YRNBH
Aggregate	-4.97	0.14
Welfare	-18.19*	-12.34
Higher Education	4.08	7.42*
Lower Education	-1.80	-0.79
Health	-0.34	3.36*
Combined Appeal	-1.38	-3.49**

*Coefficient significant at .10 or better.

**Coefficient significant at .01 or better.

is no reason to expect government social welfare spending to influence giving to, for instance, the arts or universities. Thus, the use of aggregate giving as the dependent variable will also obscure the effects of government spending policy on donations.[25]

Evidence of Free Riding

Some tentative support for the free-rider hypothesis exists (Table 6.4). In four of five equations, the coefficient for OTHGIV is negative—suggesting that the typical donor gives less as others give more—but it is significant only for giving to welfare organizations. The fact that donors may respond to giving by others has important implications for the impact of tax policy changes such as the Tax Reform Act of 1986 that are discussed in Chapter 9.

The coefficient for YRNBH is, as expected, positive. This may reflect the increased difficulty of free riding the longer one lives in a community, or it may result from increased information one acquires by living in a neighborhood for a long time. The significant negative coefficient of YRNBH in the combined appeals equation—indicating that newcomers to a neighborhood give more to united charities than oldtimers—supports this second view since combined appeals can be viewed as a response to imperfect donor information (see Chapter 4). As individuals learn more about the needs of their community, as well as the quality of various charities, they appear to switch from giving to combined appeals to giving to particular charities, such as in health and higher education. In fact, YRNBH appears to have little impact on total giving; rather, it affects the composition of that giving.

Other Determinants of Money Donations

Educational attainment appears to have a strong influence on contributions of money. Schooling may act as a socializing force, encouraging cooperative, or altruistic, behavior. Also, more highly educated people receive more solicitations from charities, thus encouraging giving.

Neither the presence of children nor the marital status of the household head appear to exert a strong influence on money donations. However women appear to give less, other things being equal.[26]

The proxies included for preferences have some explanatory power. Individuals with a strong religious background (BACK-REL = 1) give significantly more money but not to any of the types of charity examined separately here. This suggests that religious individuals give more to religious charities, but not to other sorts of organizations. In addition, those who spend more time informally helping friends and neighbors also give significantly more money, in total, to charity.[27]

SUMMARY

Empirical estimation of money donations equations indicate that charitable giving responds to economic variables, such as prices and income, and that government tax and spending policies exert strong influences on the charitable sector. Charitable contributions of money appear quite responsive to price changes induced by tax reform. Government spending influences giving as well, although in a complex way. Cuts in cash transfers to the needy, for instance, encourage donors to increase charitable giving, but reductions in government support of the charitable sector appear to lead to declines in giving.

NOTES

1. Menchik and Weisbrod (1981, 1987) constructed many of the variables used in this analysis.

2. Organization type is as reported by the donor. Note that giving to these five types of charity do not add up to total giving, since some types of charities, such as religious organizations, were not examined separately.

3. This is the "first dollar" price of a donation. Large contributions by an itemizer may pull him or her into a lower tax bracket and, so, lead to a higher price of a donation. It is also assumed here that the decision to itemize is independent of the decision of how much to contribute. Clotfelter (1980) estimates that this is not the case for approximately 6 percent of all taxpayers.

4. The construction of the NETWAGE variable is discussed in detail in Appendix A to this chapter.

5. Limiting the sample in this way could introduce a sample selection bias if the decision to be a one-earner family is endogenous to the model. However, this is not likely to be a severe problem here. If we estimated an equation explaining whether a household has a single earner or not, the error term from that equation would likely not be highly correlated with the error term in the money donations equation. Thus, observations would be randomly missing and coefficient estimates would be unbiased.

6. Smith and Rosenbaum (1981) estimate that 41 percent of federal government spending on social services in 1980 went directly to nonprofit organizations.

7. State and county of residence, and so government spending data, are available for only 1,887 of 2,802 respondents. For this reason, 915 observations were dropped from the regression analysis.

8. No definition of neighborhood is provided. The respondent implicitly defines it in his or her answer.

9. This will be the case to a greater extent for some types of charity examined here, such as social welfare, than others, such as the arts.

10. EDUC is measured as follows: 0 = no schooling; 1 = 1–6 years of schooling; 2 = 7–8 years; 3 = 9–11 years; 4 = 12 or more years (no college degree); 5 = AA degree; 6 = BA or BS; 7 = advanced degree.

11. Such giving may not be "charitable" in the usual sense, since one's own children will benefit. However, it is considered charitable if external benefits are provided. As noted in Chapter 2, we assume that all tax-deductible organizations are charitable in this sense.

12. Twelve percent reported giving no money, while 68 percent volunteered no time. The percentages are higher for the disaggregated equations.

13. See Tobin (1958) for a description of this procedure.

14. For complete regression results, see Appendix B to this chapter.

15. An elasticity measures the percentage change in one variable brought about by a 1 percent change in another variable. For example, the price elasticity of money donations is the percentage change in money donations brought about by a 1 percent change in its price.

16. For a detailed review of the econometric literature on charitable giving, see Clotfelter (1985).

17. To see this, note that donations, D, received by the charitable sector, from any individual, can be written as:

$$D = (1 - t)D + tD$$

where $(1 - t)D$ is the cost to the donor, and tD is the cost borne by the government in terms of foregone revenue. A price elasticity of -1 implies that the total cost to the donor remains constant as the price to the donor, $(1 - t)$, changes. Therefore, any increase in D brought by deductibility must be exactly matched by an increase in revenue foregone, tD. An elasticity larger in absolute value than -1 implies that deductibility increases $(1 - t)D$, so that the gain to the charitable sector exceeds the revenue lost by government. See Feldstein and Taylor (1976) for a discussion of this point.

18. See, e.g., Hochman and Rodgers (1977) for a discussion of both equity and efficiency issues involved in evaluating tax deductions and credits for charitable giving.

19. The cross-price elasticities measure the percentage change in money donations associated with a 1 percent change in the price of volunteering.

20. See Schiff (1985) for the calculations.

21. There are little data available on the extent to which state and local governments support the nonprofit sector.

22. Smith and Rosenbaum (1981, p. 48) estimate, for instance, that 41 percent of federal government spending on social services went directly to charitable organizations.

23. See Schiff (1985).

24. See, e.g., Abrams and Schmitz (1978, 1984) and Lindsey and Steinberg (1988).

25. Results for giving to types of charity other than social welfare are less dramatic and are thus not discussed in the text. However, state spending on higher education does appear to crowd out giving to higher education. See Appendix B to this chapter for complete results.

26. One should be careful when interpreting this result, since the sample includes only single-earner households. Women heading such households are probably atypical in a variety of ways.

27. Another explanation of this result is that individuals who overstate their charitable giving also overstate the time they spend helping friends and neighbors.

Appendix A: Construction of Regression Variables

A number of independent variables used in the regression analysis of Chapters 6 and 7 were constructed by Menchik and Weisbrod (1981, 1987). Here I present a discussion of that construction, which is adapted from discussions by Menchik and Weisbrod (1981).

As noted, wage rate data were unavailable from the survey. Gross wage was computed as:

$$w = (Y - \Sigma^i r^i K^i) / H$$

where:

Y is the respondent's taxable household income;

K^i is the reported value of the respondent's assets of type i;

r^i is the imputed annual rate of return on asset i;

H is the number of hours worked for pay in 1973.

Three classes of assets and corresponding rates of return were used. Dividend income was estimated as the reported value of wealth held in common stocks and mutual funds at an estimated rate of return of 3.06 percent. (This rate appears in the *Annual Statistical Digest*, Board of Governors of the Federal Reserve, Table 27, p. 126.) Interest income was estimated as the reported value of wealth held in bank accounts, certificates of deposit, bonds, and other instruments paying fixed amounts per year at a return of 6.92 percent. (This rate of return is the 1973 rate on three- to five-year U.S. government bonds.) Finally, other property income was estimated as the reported amounts invested in unincorporated businesses, private corporations, and real estate at an estimated return of 3.06 percent.

Total asset income in all three forms was subtracted from reported gross income to obtain an estimate of earnings, and this was divided by reported hours of work to obtain a gross wage rate, w. Full income (INCOME) was then obtained by subtracting the estimate of labor earnings, wH, from reported income from all sources, and then adding imputed rental income from owner-occupied housing and wH^*, where H^* was chosen to be 2,000 hours, the approximate number worked annually by a full-time worker. Imputed rental income was calculated as the product of the reported value of homes owned and 9.11 percent, a weighted average of annual rent-to-housing values computed in the national income accounts.

The net-of-tax wage rate, NETWAGE, was determined by computing the marginal tax rate consistent with each respondent's INCOME, marital status, family size, itemization status, and the estimated amount of income that would qualify for the dividend exclusion. Itemizers were assumed to deduct the mean amount for their income class (there were twenty-five classes). For non-itemizers, the standard deduction was 0.15 times the adjusted gross income up to $2,000. Marginal tax rates were determined from the tax tables, with married taxpayers assumed to file jointly and single taxpayers assumed to be household heads. NET-WAGE is equal to $w(1 - t)$, where t is the estimated marginal tax rate on earnings.

The price of a money donation, PRICE, is calculated as 1 for non-itemizers and $(1 - t')$ for itemizers, where t' is the marginal tax rate on all income. While PRICE and NETWAGE are both functions of marginal tax rates, they are not perfectly correlated, for three reasons. First, non-itemizers typically face a positive tax rate on earnings, t, but t' is, in effect, zero in PRICE. Second, the maximum t was 50 percent, but t' can exceed 50 percent. Finally, people may have the same INCOME but may differ in its composition between earnings and unearned income, so that PRICE and NETWAGE can vary independently.

Appendix B: Regression Results

Table A6.1
Means and Standard Deviations of Variables

Variable	Mean	Standard Deviation
Independent Variables:		
PRICE	0.85	0.15
INCOME	21300.00	42328.00
NETWAGE	5.74	10.10
LCITY	0.13	0.38
MCITY	0.18	0.38
SCITY	0.31	0.46
SUBCITY	0.19	0.39
BACKGIV	0.79	0.41
BACKREL	0.73	0.44
BACKED	0.34	0.47
HELPER	75.61	157.30
YGKID	0.26	0.44
OTHKID	0.38	0.49
YRNBH	12.22	14.66
EDUC	4.57	1.49
WHITE	0.89	0.31
AGE	41.84	12.89
PERPOOR	9.56	6.64
PCINC	4.94	0.65
FEMALE	0.31	0.46
MARRIED	0.64	0.48
OTHGIV	67.16	14.60
Government Spending:		
STATEGOV	791.56	143.49
WELFARE	112.50	76.06
CASH	56.16	33.00
HIED	119.86	37.79
LOWED	333.04	50.01
HOSP	78.33	23.30
HEALTH	25.81	7.53
LOCGOV	246.01	85.35
LOCSW	15.10	19.83
Contributions of Money:		
AGGREGATE	483.68	1868.50
WELFARE	5.16	75.03
HIGHER ED.	8.73	76.42
LOWER ED.	5.42	72.79
HEALTH	15.53	108.55
COMBINED APPEAL	28.42	141.64

Table A6.1 (continued)

Variable	Mean	Standard Deviation
Contributions of Time:		
AGGREGATE	56.23	172.16
WELFARE	3.16	42.23
HIGHER ED.	0.77	8.62
LOWER ED.	3.07	40.10
HEALTH	5.03	57.05
COMBINED APPEAL	0.46	6.53
FUNDRAISING	3.83	26.90
LEADERSHIP	14.35	69.70
CLERICAL/MANUAL	7.74	45.78
TEACHING	13.32	79.06
PROFESSIONAL	8.43	66.79
COUNSELING	5.31	46.16

Table A6.2
Donations of Money: Tobit Regression Results[a]

			Equation			
Independent Variables	Aggregate	Welfare	Health	Higher Ed	Lower Ed	Combined Appeal
PRICE	-5429.50	-1026.84	-912.29	-815.61	-5177.17	-599.02
	(5.96)	(1.18)	(3.42)	(1.54)	(2.16)	(2.97)
INCOME	.059	.004	.004	.002	.003	.007
	(4.78)	(0.52)	(1.57)	(0.45)	(0.21)	(3.38)
NETWAGE	-248.41	-82.23	-20.84	-10.12	-8.52	-36.53
	(4.97)	(1.78)	(1.82)	(0.47)	(0.16)	(3.54)
LCITY	811.02	143.83	72.42	379.91	-350.19	228.14
	(2.08)	(0.62)	(0.59)	(1.56)	(0.44)	(2.77)
MCITY	220.84	-235.82	157.45	-324.86	534.86	60.98
	(0.59)	(0.86)	(1.33)	(1.05)	(0.97)	(0.73)
SCITY	-97.95	-79.30	162.65	-25.03	-181.80	75.24
	(0.30)	(0.35)	(1.52)	(0.11)	(0.36)	(0.95)
SUBCITY	121.96	-11.65	195.19	-13.15	-565.50	143.73
	(0.32)	(0.05)	(1.68)	(0.06)	(0.86)	(1.79)
BACKGIVE	177.78	-255.28	146.94	62.20	5430.93	11.51
	(0.66)	(1.47)	(1.68)	(0.33)	(0.02)	(0.21)
BACKREL	466.06	270.25	-52.31	-79.97	106.05	-42.86
	(1.89)	(1.49)	(0.79)	(0.58)	(0.12)	(0.91)
BACKED	94.86	135.29	61.84	260.77	-459.37	8.97
	(0.41)	(0.87)	(1.01)	(2.02)	(1.14)	(0.20)
HELPER	1.99	-0.09	0.33	-0.41	0.32	-0.01
	(3.15)	(0.19)	(2.18)	(0.79)	(0.24)	(0.06)
YGKID	2.92	68.00	42.02	-95.10	580.05	-9.11
	(0.01)	(0.34)	(0.30)	(0.54)	(1.00)	(0.15)
OTHKID	345.17	173.61	84.31	-85.83	238.87	-35.29
	(1.24)	(1.05)	(1.29)	(0.61)	(0.64)	(0.74)
YRNBH	0.14	-12.34	3.36	7.42	0.79	-3.61
	(0.02)	(1.52)	(1.78)	(1.73)	(0.07)	(2.00)
EDUC	226.13	114.84	57.84	193.53	117.90	49.78
	(2.79)	(1.95)	(2.63)	(3.51)	(0.82)	(3.15)
WHITE	93.56	-60.43	-26.40	28.70	3453.25	-35.12
	(0.26)	(0.25)	(0.24)	(0.02)	(0.01)	(0.49)
AGE	25.59	72.83	28.73	43.34	33.75	24.48
	(0.40)	(1.42)	(1.49)	(0.94)	(0.24)	(1.84)
AGE^2	-0.15	-0.67	-0.30	-0.51	0.06	0.20
	(0.02)	(1.20)	(1.42)	(1.00)	(0.05)	(1.38)
PERPOOR	-1.52	13.85	2.17	-61.43	50.07	-11.64
	(0.08)	(1.28)	(0.40)	(2.03)	(2.00)	(2.11)

Table A6.2 (continued)

Independent Variables	Equation					
	Aggregate	Welfare	Health	Higher Ed	Lower Ed	Combined Appeal
PCINC	-38.31	104.31	-42.27	-128.38	739.50	14.46
	(0.15)	(0.50)	(0.62)	(0.68)	(0.40)	(0.29)
FEMALE	-505.56	132.06	33.44	41.56	256.45	-196.81
	(1.80)	(0.69)	(0.44)	(0.25)	(0.45)	(3.32)
MARRIED	57.24	294.41	61.87	141.03	-42.27	39.60
	(0.20)	(1.41)	(0.76)	(0.76)	(0.79)	(0.67)
OTHGIV	-4.97	-18.19	-0.34	4.08	-1.80	-1.33
	(0.60)	(1.95)	(0.17)	(0.64)	(0.07)	(0.78)
STATEGOV	3.96					0.16
	(2.73)					(0.59)
WELFARE		7.37				
		(2.50)				
CASH		-9.32				
		(2.46)				
HIED				-3.43	3.95	
				(1.90)	(0.70)	
LOWED				0.10	0.28	
				(0.03)	(0.04)	
HOSP			-0.98			
			(0.72)			
HEALTH			-1.92			
			(0.42)			
LOCGOV	-7.62		-0.06	0.98	-3.51	-0.30
	(2.94)		(0.11)	(0.72)	(0.83)	(0.61)
LOCSW		5.55				
		(1.19)				
CONSTANT	356.07	-242.77	-629.31	-4426.81	-13201.90	-618.70
	(0.15)	(1.34)	(0.92)	(0.01)	(0.01)	(1.29)
1/s	.0004	.0017	.0026	.0020	.0014	.0029

Note: the number of observations for these equations is 734.

[a]T-statistics in parentheses.

7.

Volunteering: Empirical Evidence

INTRODUCTION

In this chapter, the *National Survey of Philanthropy* is used to estimate volunteer supply equations, analogous to the money donations equations estimated in Chapter 6, and to test the predictions made by each of the models of volunteering. Since each of the models of volunteering presented in Chapter 5 probably describes only one aspect of volunteer behavior, it should come as no surprise that the results do not allow us to discover a single motive for giving time. They do, however, provide evidence of the relative importance of each model, particularly for different volunteer activities. In addition, the results allow for estimates of the effects of changes in government fiscal policies on donations of time.

Implications of the Models of Volunteering

The "collective goods" model of volunteering predicts results similar to those for money donations. In particular, changes in government spending would affect money and time donations in similar ways. Also, because money and time are given for the same reason, the two types of donations would be perfect substitutes.

When a private motive for volunteering is introduced into the analysis, predictions are modified somewhat. Donations of money and time are still expected to be substitutes, but perhaps only weakly. The effect of government spending policy on volunteering would be qualitatively similar to its impact on money donations but, again, the impact will be less pronounced.

The influence and search models predict that hours donated depend, in part, on a person's ability to influence output type or gather information as well as the value, to him or her, of that influence or information. Money and time donations may be complements in these models. The impact of government spending policy on volunteering is complicated by the fact that the demand for influence or information does not vary in a simple way with the demand for charitable output. In addition, government support of the charitable sector may provide information, or limit the scope for volunteer influence, and so may discourage donations of time.

Finally, if individuals volunteer in order to acquire skills which increase their future wages, donations of time will be greatest for those with the ability to acquire job skills easily and to turn those skills into higher future wages. So, volunteering should rise with education and fall with age. Money and time donations should have little relationship in this case, and there seems to be little reason to expect government spending policies to affect volunteering.

DATA AND EXPECTED RESULTS

Dependent Variables

I estimate equations for aggregate volunteering as well as for volunteering to particular types of charity. In addition, I estimate separate equations for particular volunteer activities. In the aggregate equation, the dependent variable is the self-reported total number of hours volunteered to all organizations in 1973. The types of charities for which I estimate separate volunteer equations are the same as for the money equations. Finally, the types of volunteer activities examined—again self-reported—are: fundraising, leadership, clerical or manual, teaching, professional, and counseling. Breaking volunteering into particular activities will aid in distinguishing between different motives for giving.

Explanatory Variables

The same set of explanatory variables is employed as in the money donations equations. However, the expectations regarding coefficients will be different and the interpretation more difficult, since there are several competing models.

Prices and Income

The price of volunteering in the empirical model is NET-WAGE. I expect a negative coefficient for NETWAGE regardless of which model of volunteering holds. One complication, however, is that NETWAGE may reflect, in addition to the donor's opportunity cost of time, his or her productivity as a volunteer—either in terms of output produced, influence wielded, or information gathered. Workers who are especially productive in their paying jobs, and so earn high wages, may be better volunteers, and thus may have greater incentive to give time. This effect would tend to offset the effect of a higher opportunity cost of time.[1]

If people are unable to work their optimal number of hours, NETWAGE will not be a perfect measure of the opportunity cost of time. Marital status and number of children in the household may, in this case, influence the cost of volunteering.[2] Married individuals may have a lower opportunity cost of volunteering because a spouse can watch the children, cook, clean the house, etc. We would expect, therefore, a positive coefficient for MARRIED.

Individuals with children will find it more costly to give up time in order to volunteer. On the other hand, volunteering for particular types of charity, such as educational institutions, will likely rise with the presence of children since demand for the services of such organizations, and for influence over those services, will increase.[3]

The variable PRICE here enters the equations as a cross price. The coefficient will be positive if money and time donations are substitutes and negative if they are complements. We expect that money donations are more likely to be complementary with those types of activities, such as volunteer leadership, which allow the greatest opportunity for influence. In the money equations, the two types of contributions were generally complements. The results need not be symmetric, however, since the volunteering induced by a lower NETWAGE provides information, while money donations brought about by a fall in PRICE do not.

Income will likely have a positive effect on volunteering, since the "goods" acquired by volunteering all appear to be normal.

Government Expenditures

The government spending variables reflect both government output and government support for the charitable sector. The interpretation of the results is complicated by the fact that there are several competing models of volunteering.

The collective goods model of volunteering predicts that aggregate hours donated will respond to changes in STATEGOV and LOCGOV in much the same manner as aggregate money donations. Recall that contributions of money rise as local government budgets are cut but fall with reductions in state spending.

In the equation for vounteering to welfare organizations, CASH reflects only government transfers to the needy and not grants to charities. Thus, the coefficient for CASH provides information about the strength of the collective output motive for volunteering.

If donors are motivated by the desire for influence, then a cut in government output may lead donors to switch from volunteering to donating money, as increasing charitable output becomes more valuable relative to gaining influence. Cuts in government support to the charitable sector will, besides influencing demand for charitable output, tend to make it easier for volunteers to influence output type. The more free the charitable sector is from government intervention, the greater reliance on volunteers we would expect. Government support of the charitable sector also provides information to potential donors, lessening the need for volunteering-as-search. Thus, cuts in such support should again encourage volunteering.

Finally, the job training model predicts no significant relationship between government expenditures and volunteering.

I deal with the relative importance of each of these motivations for volunteering by comparing the impact of changes in government spending on various volunteer activities. Those activities—such as leadership—that allow for significant influence or information gathering may respond much more positively to cuts in the level of government support of the charitable sector than other activities—such as clerical or manual labor—which do not appear to allow for much influence or information, but rather fit more easily into the collective goods model.

Note, finally, that the results for volunteering should be viewed in conjunction with those for money donations (Chapter 6). Certain changes, such as cuts in government grants to the charitable sector, may make volunteering more attractive relative to money donations. We may, then, see a shift from one form of giving to the other.

Free-Rider Behavior

To the extent that individuals volunteer in order to increase charitable output, they may free ride on either money or time donations by others. The coefficient for OTHGIV would, then, be negative.[4] In addition, volunteers would increase volunteering as YRNBH increases and as community size falls. Those volunteers seeking information or influence will have a more difficult time free riding on other volunteers and will be unable to free ride on money donors at all.

State and Local Socioeconomic Variables

The collective goods model predicts that donations of time respond to the socioeconomic variables in much the same way as contributions of money. The implications of the influence and search models depend, as in the case of government expenditures, on the relationship between demand for influence and information and demand for output. The job training model predicts no relationship—an individual's desire to acquire job skills

Table 7.1
Estimated Price and Income Elasticities of Volunteering by Type of Charity

Type of Charity	Elasticities		
	Price	Income	Cross-Price
Aggregate	-0.11	0.14	-0.36
Welfare	0.86	0.66	0.90
Higher Education	-3.43	1.08	-8.43
Lower Education	-2.64**	0.39	-7.01*
Health	-0.52	0.48	-5.39**
Combined Appeal	-1.57*	1.46**	2.86

*Coefficient significant at .10 or better.

**Coefficient significant at .01 or better.

should have little to do with the well-being of others in his or her state or county.

RESULTS BY TYPE OF CHARITY[5]

Price and Income Elasticities

Contributions of time, both in the aggregate and to particular types of charity, appear to be less price and income elastic than donations of money. As indicated in Table 7.1, the price elasticity[6] is negative and significant for only two of the five types of charity examined and is not significantly different from zero for aggregate volunteering. This would seem to suggest that volunteering is fairly unresponsive to changes in the opportunity cost of time. Recall, however, that NETWAGE may also reflect a donor's productivity as a volunteer. So, those facing a high cost of volunteering may also have the most to gain by giving time.

Children may increase the opportunity cost of time and, at the same time, increase parents' demands for certain charitable output or for influence over that output. Both of these effects appear to operate. The presence of children age six to seventeen increases total volunteering (the coefficient for OTHKID is positive and significant), largely because of an increase in hours donated to lower education. Thus, the impact of older children on demand for charitable output seems to have a greater influence on volunteering than does their effect on the opportunity cost of the parents' time.

The presence of children less than six years old has little effect on aggregate volunteering (the coefficient is positive but not significant) although there is some weak evidence of a movement toward giving time to lower education (the coefficient for YGKID is positive but not significant for lower education). Finally young children have a more negative impact on volunteering than older children. This is expected; younger children generally require more care and attention and thus imply a higher opportunity cost of time for parents.[7]

The estimated cross-price elasticity is generally negative, indicating that money and time donations are complements, but is significant only for volunteering to lower education and health. The weakness of this cross-price effect, relative to that for money donations, is not surprising; gifts of money, encouraged by a fall in PRICE, do not generate information for donors, as does volunteering.

Finally, the income elasticity is positive, but significantly different from zero only for combined appeals.

Volunteering and Government Spending

Aggregate volunteering does not appear to be affected by government expenditure policy. As indicated in Table 7.2, the coefficients on STATEGOV and LOCGOV are very close to zero and insignificant. This is in contrast to money donations, in which both state and local spending had significant impact on giving. Given the mixed predictions of the various models, this weak result is not unexpected.

The case of volunteering for social welfare organizations is quite different, however, and is instructive for understanding the

Table 7.2
Elasticities of Hours Donated with Respect to Per Capita Government Expenditures

Type of Expenditure	Type of Charity[a]	
	Aggregate	Welfare
STATEGOV	-0.04	
LOCGOV	-0.03	
CASH		4.75*
WELFARE		-4.96*
LOCSW		-0.27

[a]Results for other types of charity are presented in the Appendix to this chapter.

*Coefficient significant at .10 or better.

differences between money and time donations. Volunteer labor donated to welfare organizations falls as cash transfers (CASH) are cut but increases as other welfare spending is reduced.

These results are in the opposite direction as those for money donations and of approximately equal quantitative significance. A one-dollar fall in CASH would lead to an 0.25 hour fall in per capita volunteering, while a dollar reduction in WELFARE would encourage volunteering to rise by 0.13 hours per person. These results suggest that changes in government expenditure policy will affect both the level of charitable giving and the mix between gifts of money and time.

The results can be viewed in terms of the effects of government intervention in the charity market. A cut in cash transfers represents a reduction in government output only, with no change in the level of government support for charities. Such a spending cut will, as long as charity substitutes for cash transfers—and the results for money donations suggest that it does—increase demand for charitable output. As this demand increases, donors appear to switch from volunteering to money donations. Money donations are more productive than volunteering in terms of producing output, but volunteering can provide other collective benefits, such as influence and certain private gains. When demand for charitable output is high, the advantages of giving money are dominant, and the mix of contributions shifts away from time and toward money.

On the other hand, as government support for charities—a major component of WELFARE—decreases, the scope for volunteer influence and the need for information gathering both rise, and donors switch from giving money to volunteering.

Volunteering, Information, and Free Riding

Potential volunteers will be able to free ride on the money donations of others only to the extent that volunteers are motivated by the desire to increase charitable output. Results provide no evidence of such free riding—the coefficient of OTHGIV is insignificant in all six cases, and positive in five of the six.

People do appear to volunteer more, both in the aggregate and specifically to health organizations and combined appeals, the longer they live in a community.[8]

Volunteering and Attitudes Toward Philanthropy

We saw in the previous chapter that proxies for attitudes toward giving play an important role in explaining differences in giving of money. These attitudes do not, however, appear to have much influence on volunteering. Individuals from religious backgrounds (BACKREL = 1) do not volunteer more or less than others in total, although they do give more time to lower education (which most likely represents giving to religious schools). This contrasts the result that those from religious backgrounds do give more money in total. In addition, those who spend more time informally helping friends and neighbors (HELPER) do not volunteer more than others, again in contrast to the results for money donations. The fact that the proxies for attitudes toward philanthropy play a much less important role in explaining volunteering than money donations suggests that private motives—such as job training or the ability to interact socially with other volunteers—may play an important role in determining hours volunteered.

Evidence on Volunteering as Job Training

The job training model of volunteering predicts that the number of hours an individual volunteers depends on the cost of volunteering, the person's ability to acquire and take advantage of job skills, and the number of years over which he or she can take advantage of those skills. The results, by charity, provide only limited support for this model; the effect of education is positive and generally significant. However, when we examine results for specific volunteer activities, we will find much stronger evidence for the notion that many volunteers are, in fact, motivated by the desire to gain job skills.[9]

Volunteering by Charity: Summary

The preceding analysis paints a somewhat confusing picture of the economics of volunteering. There is evidence, first, that volunteers are less concerned with increasing charitable output than are money donors. Government spending has a very different impact on volunteering than on contributions of money, one that suggests that donors view contributions of money, rather than time, as the preferred means for increasing charitable output, while volunteering may be seen as a means for obtaining influence or information. In addition, philanthropic attitudes explain little about volunteer behavior.

RESULTS FOR VOLUNTEERING BY ACTIVITY

Volunteers perform a wide variety of tasks—from leadership of a charity to clerical or manual tasks. By aggregating these various activities, I may have combined volunteers with very different motivations, and so obscured evidence of each motivation. Here I estimate volunteer equations for seven activities:[10] leadership, counseling, professional, teaching, fundrais-

Table 7.3
Estimated Price and Income Elasticities of Volunteering by Type of Volunteer Activity

Type of Activity	Elasticities		
	Price	Income	Cross-Price
Leadership	-0.57	0.31	-3.08**
Teaching	-0.15	0.25	1.62
Professional	-1.40	1.04	0.45
Counseling	0.52	-0.60	-0.10
Fundraising	-0.39	0.01	-2.23*
Clerical/Manual	0.95*	-0.83	0.10
Helper	-0.09	0.09	2.48

*Coefficient significant at .10 or better.

**Coefficient significant at .01 or better.

ing, clerical or manual, and HELPER (informal volunteering not done via an organization).[11] Each of the models of volunteering presented are applicable to some activities but not others.

Prices and Income

Table 7.3 presents price and income elasticities for each volunteer activity. The estimated cross-price elasticities are of particular interest. Money donations are most complementary with volunteer leadership—results suggest that a 1 percent fall in the price of a money donation will, other things being equal, increase volunteer leadership by over 3 percent. Volunteer leaders will have more influence over the activities of an organization than those engaged in other volunteer activities. Therefore, when the price of a money donation falls, encouraging contributions of cash, those wishing to complement their money donations with influence will undertake activities such as leadership.[12]

Fundraising is also a complement of money donations. This is more difficult to explain; there is little reason to believe that fundraisers wield much influence over, or gain much information about, a charity's activities.

At the other extreme, informal volunteering (HELPER) appears to be a substitute for giving money (although the coefficient is not significant). This makes intuitive sense as well, since informal volunteering does not buy influence over any charitable organization.

None of the volunteer activities appear to be responsive to the opportunity cost of time, as measured by NETWAGE. As noted, however, the presence of children may affect the cost of volunteering and also influence demand for charitable output. Results indicate that volunteer teaching, fundraising, and clerical or manual labor all rise with the presence of an older child (OTH-KID = 1). Thus, it appears that, for these activities, the demand effect outweighs the impact of any increased opportunity cost of time. HELPER, on the other hand, falls with the presence of children. The demand for aid to friends and neighbors should not be influenced by the presence of children, leaving only the negative effect on HELPER of increased opportunity cost. On the other hand, the output produced by volunteer teaching is consumed by children, so that the demand effect is strong.

Government Spending, Influence, and Volunteer Activities

Four of the volunteer activities—leadership, clerical or manual, counseling, and HELPER—are hypothesized to depend on state and local social welfare expenditures, as measured by state cash transfers to the needy, CASH, other state social welfare spending, WELFARE, and local government spending on social welfare, LOCSW.[13] For each of these activities, the coefficient signs are the same, and estimated elasticities are quite similar (Table 7.4). Each of these volunteer activities increases with CASH (significant in three of four cases), decreases as WEL-

FARE rises (significant in two of four) and decreases with LOCSW (significant in one case).

These results can again be interpreted in terms of the influence argument. Government support of the charitable sector, by reducing the potential scope for volunteer influence, tends to reduce volunteering.[14] The coefficients for both WELFARE and LOCSW reflect, in part, the effect of government support of the charitable sector, while that for CASH reflects only the impact on demand for charitable output. The results indicate that a cut in cash transfers, which presumably increases demand for charity, would lead to a fall in each of these four volunteer activities, as donors switched to giving money. However, a reduction in WELFARE or LOCSW would lead to an increase in these activities, as volunteers take advantage of increased opportunities for influence or desire for information.

In addition, one would expect that leadership is a "high influence" activity and we find, in fact, that it declines most sharply as WELFARE and LOCSW rise. Other activities that appear to provide less influence, such as clerical or manual, are less affected by changes in such government spending.[15]

Professional volunteering was hypothesized to be a function of spending on health, measured by spending on hospitals (HOSP) and other health-related spending (HEALTH).[16] Such volunteer activity increases if states cut their health spending. Volunteer teaching would, similarly, rise in response to lower education budget cuts.

Free Riding and Demonstration Effects

Free riding does not appear to take place for most activities. The coefficient for OTHGIV is negative for only two of the seven activities and is significant only for clerical or manual. The fact that clerical or manual volunteer labor is more responsive to money donations by others than are other activities is perhaps not surprising, given that clerical or manual would appear to fit best the collective goods model of volunteering.

On the other hand, demonstration effects appear to dominate for professional activities; the coefficient for OTHGIV is positive and significant. Professionals may be motivated to volunteer

Table 7.4
Elasticities of Hours Donated with Respect to Government Spending by Type of Volunteer Activity

Type of Expenditure	Volunteer Activity:			
	Fundraising	Leadership	Clerical/ Manual	Teaching
STATEGOV	-1.98			
WELFARE		-1.43*	-0.91	
CASH		1.46**	1.25**	
HIED				0.85
LOWED				-4.38*
HOSP				
HEALTH				
LOCGOV	1.36			0.17
LOCSW		-0.34*	-0.15	

*Coefficient significant at .10 or better.

**Coefficient significant at .01 or better.

in order to gain acceptance or prestige within their community. This is also consistent with the result that professional as well as teaching time increase significantly the longer one lives in a neighborhood.

Evidence of Volunteering as Job Training

Certain volunteer activities seem, a priori, to involve far more important elements of job training than others. For instance, informal volunteering, HELPER, should have no effect on future wages, so that results for HELPER should not reflect the influences of age and education discussed above. Performing clerical

Table 7.4 (continued)

| Type of Expenditure | Volunteer Activity: | | |
	Professional	Counseling	HELPER
STATEGOV			
WELFARE		-1.16	-1.13**
CASH		1.06	0.95**
HIED			
LOWED			
HOSP	0.81		
HEALTH	-3.25**		
LOCGOV	0.60		
LOCSW		-0.02	-0.08

*Coefficient significant at .10 or better.

**Coefficient significant at .01 or better.

or manual tasks for a charity will, similarly, provide little in the way of job training.

Volunteer leadership, on the other hand, should have a relatively large impact on future wages, due to the skills acquired and personal contacts made in such an activity, as well as on the value of the activity as a signal to potential employers. Therefore, the predictions of the training model should be well supported for leadership. Other volunteer activities—teaching, counseling, fundraising, and professional work—also appear to provide some training and/or value as a signal, although perhaps to a lesser extent than leadership.

The predictions of the job training model are most strongly supported by the equations for volunteer leadership and teaching (Table 7.5). For each, the coefficient for AGE is positive and

Table 7.5
Evidence of the Job Training Model of Volunteering by Activity
(coefficients on AGE, AGE², EDUC and FEMALE)

Type of Activity	AGE	AGE^2	EDUC	FEMALE
Leadership	26.82**	-0.31**	39.47**	-99.47*
Teaching	44.27**	-0.55**	63.02**	2.23
Professional	16.45	-0.25	79.36*	-32.81
Counseling	-7.77	0.03	41.34**	69.47
Fundraising	2.79	0.03	-2.66	23.57
Clerical/Manual	0.42	.004	6.67	59.50**
Helper	-0.47	-0.02	2.57	22.65

*Coefficient significant at .10 or better.

**Coefficient significant at .01 or better.

significant, and that for AGE squared (AGE^2) is negative and significant, implying that volunteering rises and then falls with age.[17] The implied turning point, at which volunteering begins to decline, is thirty-three years for professional and forty for teaching. Other activities with seemingly less important training components—such as HELPER and clerical or manual—show no relationship with age.

In addition, hours volunteered rise significantly with education for both of these activities, which may reflect the ability of more highly educated individuals to acquire skills more rapidly and to take advantage of those skills more fully. Education is not a significant variable in the equations for fundraising, clerical or manual, or HELPER—precisely those activities that one would not expect investment in job skills to play an important role.

Finally, women serve less frequently than men in volunteer leadership roles but more frequently as clerical or manual workers. This would be predicted within the context of the investment model if women are less able—due, for instance, to labor market discrimination— to "cash in" on skills acquired via volunteering. The same result could arise, however, from discrimination within the charitable sector.

Volunteering by Activity: Summary

Examination of specific volunteer activities makes clear a number of relationships that were obscured in the aggregate analysis and enables us to sort among the various models of volunteering. Each of these models appears to have relevance for some, but not all, volunteer activities.

Volunteer leadership appears to fit both the influence and job skills models fairly well. The impact of government spending on leadership, and the fact that such volunteering is a complement of money donations, is consistent with the notion that volunteer leaders are motivated by the desire for influence.[18] On the other hand, the impact of age and education suggests that the acquisition of job skills motivates some volunteer leaders.

Volunteer teaching appears motivated by the desire to increase charitable output—here education— and to increase future wages. The fact that people with children teach more and that volunteer teaching increases as government spending on education falls each suggest that volunteer teachers conform to the collective goods model. The results for age and education again support the job training model.

Clerical or manual and informal volunteering (HELPER) fit the collective goods model fairly closely and do not fit the other explanations of volunteering well at all. Both are substitutes for money donations, as the collective goods model predicts, and those with children donate more clerical or manual labor.

The voluntary supply of professional labor increases with cuts in government health budgets, suggesting that the collective goods model is relevant. There is also some evidence that professional labor is volunteered in order to gain prestige or conform to social pressure, since hours donated rise with both YRNBH and OTHGIV. Finally, volunteer counseling is not well explained by any of these models.

NOTES

1. Note that education level is included as an explanatory variable. To the extent that this controls for differences in productivity as a volunteer, NETWAGE will reflect only the opportunity cost.

2. Recall that in the money equations marital status and dummies for the presence of children were hypothesized to have a potential effect on the demand for charitable output. Here they may have that effect as well as an effect on the value of one's time.

3. Demand for information about such organizations may also rise although, as noted in Chapter 5, it need not.

4. Data on volunteering by others are, unfortunately, not available.

5. For complete regression results, see the Appendix to this chapter. The empirical results in this section represent an extension of the work by Menchik and Weisbrod (1981, 1987).

6. Note that in the volunteering equations, the price elasticity is obtained from the coefficient for NETWAGE, while the cross-price elasticity is obtained from the coefficient for PRICE.

7. Young children may also consume less charitable output. For instance, they are less likely to attend schools at which parents may volunteer.

8. The coefficient for YRNBH in the aggregate equation is not significant at .10, but it is nearly so.

9. Mueller (1975) also examines the job training motive for volunteering. Utilizing a sample of college graduate women, she finds that those women planning to return to the labor force in the near future are more likely to volunteer than those with no such plans.

10. These activities are as self-reported by respondents.

11. Recall that HELPER was an independent variable in previous equations.

12. Another explanation is that individuals are designated as philanthropic leaders as an honorific reward in response to large money donations.

13. Regressions were also run in which the spending variables were total state and local spending. Results are presented in the Appendix to this chapter.

14. Government support of a charity will also affect donor demand for charitable output, although the direction of the effect is uncertain.

15. These results could also be consistent with the search model of volunteering.

16. It was assumed, in this context, that "professional" referred mainly to medical professionals. The professional volunteer labor supply was

also estimated with total state and local spending as explanatory variables. See the Appendix to this chapter for the results.

17. The skills model predicts that volunteering will fall with age. In the empirical model both AGE and AGE^2 were included to account for the fact that age may, in part, reflect differences in preferences, so that there may be a range of age over which volunteering rises.

18. Either of these results could also be interpreted in terms of the search model. However, volunteering does not fall, as the search model predicts, the longer one lives in a neighborhood.

Appendix: Regression Results

Table A7.1
Donations of Time by Type of Charity: Tobit Regression Results[a]

Independent Variables	Equation					
	Aggregate	Welfare	Combined Appeal	Higher Ed	Lower Ed	Health
PRICE	-88.40	255.63	95.55	-137.49	-680.68	-481.14
	(0.67)	(0.33)	(1.04)	(0.80)	(1.86)	(2.18)
INCOME	0.001	-0.007	0.002	0.001	0.002	0.002
	(0.76)	(0.94)	(2.37)	(0.51)	(0.61)	(0.69)
NETWAGE	3.82	32.02	-7.76	-8.32	-38.07	-6.95
	(0.52)	(0.54)	(1.75)	(0.97)	(2.14)	(0.71)
LCITY	116.12	-438.08	35.16	27.10	-163.18	92.85
	(2.00)	(1.73)	(0.90)	(0.53)	(1.28)	(0.77)
MCITY	58.30	-647.78	37.13	-55.44	-25.10	13.50
	(1.04)	(2.15)	(1.03)	(1.03)	(0.26)	(0.11)
SCITY	51.81	-586.73	-2.72	-70.85	-1.17	94.47
	(1.03)	(2.25)	(0.07)	(1.48)	(0.01)	(0.87)
SUBCITY	8.13	-491.02	6.84	-34.14	-83.42	35.19
	(0.14)	(1.72)	(0.18)	(0.71)	(0.83)	(0.29)
BACKGIVE	-6.64	64.15	-39.00	-2.37	-130.70	-25.93
	(0.17)	(0.28)	(1.77)	(0.05)	(1.86)	(0.36)
BACKREL	-1.36	-235.91	-15.25	15.25	165.81	78.22
	(0.04)	(1.24)	(0.73)	(0.43)	(2.18)	(1.11)
BACKED	18.25	63.90	28.82	38.14	151.73	103.45
	(0.54)	(0.33)	(1.34)	(1.23)	(2.49)	(1.73)
HELPER	0.09	-1.62	0.35	-0.03	0.02	0.22
	(0.97)	(1.06)	(1.60)	(0.34)	(0.10)	(1.66)
YGKID	39.18	-31.94	-16.12	-35.06	71.10	-200.78
	(0.93)	(0.02)	(0.56)	(0.81)	(0.93)	(1.95)
OTHKID	91.32	-77.29	34.85	-9.22	171.63	-52.38
	(2.59)	(0.35)	(1.58)	(0.27)	(2.57)	(0.76)
YRNBH	1.91	-12.30	1.98	0.84	0.86	3.66
	(1.62)	(1.00)	(3.60)	(0.80)	(0.43)	(2.00)
EDUC	43.12	106.41	16.38	34.04	66.12	59.79
	(3.72)	(1.60)	(1.93)	(2.43)	(2.78)	(2.87)
WHITE	51.89	147.48	-17.15	583.37	-90.51	1898.11
	(0.98)	(0.55)	(0.20)	(0.01)	(0.91)	(0.01)
AGE	12.83	-30.82	77.05	6.90	3.20	-11.82
	(1.31)	(0.65)	(1.08)	(0.64)	(0.17)	(0.76)
AGE^2	-0.16	0.27	-0.09	-0.10	0.003	0.10
	(1.49)	(0.52)	(1.19)	(0.77)	(0.01)	(0.58)
PERPOOR	-5.97	-19.52	-10.19	-1.05	-4.29	-7.76
	(1.96)	(0.90)	(1.91)	(0.26)	(0.74)	(1.25)
PCINC	-34.46	-421.28	-4.95	74.31	38.89	-16.46
	(0.95)	(1.65)	(0.17)	(1.86)	(0.55)	(0.24)

Table A7.1 (continued)

Independent Variables	Equation					
	Aggregate	Welfare	Combined Appeal	Higher Ed	Lower Ed	Health
FEMALE	39.57	192.76	-8.89	30.62	42.45	104.63
	(0.98)	(1.03)	(0.28)	(0.75)	(0.50)	(1.62)
MARRIED	-19.75	-17.88	18.55	14.83	-19.77	-80.60
	(0.45)	(0.08)	(0.53)	(0.33)	(0.22)	(1.12)
OTHGIV	0.53	0.80	-0.76	0.44	1.12	1.84
	(0.45)	(0.17)	(0.64)	(0.32)	(0.49)	(0.93)
STATEGOV	-0.01		-0.20			
	(0.05)		(1.46)			
WELFARE		-8.79				
		(1.71)				
CASH		15.76				
		(1.86)				
HIED				0.02		
				(0.04)		
LOWED					-0.03	
					(0.03)	
HOSP						1.31
						(1.05)
HEALTH						-4.91
						(1.11)
LOCGOV	-0.03		0.43	-0.35	-0.37	-0.93
	(0.08)		(1.81)	(1.32)	(0.65)	(1.57)
LOCSW		3.15				
		(0.46)				
CONSTANT	-483.66	1324.04	-265.55	-1270.50	-449.44	-1851.36
	(1.41)	(0.66)	(1.02)	(0.01)	(0.63)	(0.01)
1/s	.003	.002	.018	.010	.004	.004

Note: the number of observations for each equation is 734.

[a]T-statistics in parentheses.

Table A7.2
Donations of Time by Type of Volunteer Activity: Tobit Regression Results[a]

Independent Variables	Fund-raising	Leadership	Clerical/ Manual	Teaching	Profes-sional	Counsel-ing	Helper
PRICE	-136.32	-448.30	9.18	295.97	92.09	-13.38	61.86
	(1.66)	(2.43)	(0.10)	(1.22)	(0.17)	(0.06)	(0.87)
INCOME	0.001	0.002	-0.003	-0.002	0.009	-0.003	0.001
	(0.04)	(0.92)	(1.55)	(0.52)	(1.47)	(0.71)	(0.50)
NETWAGE	-3.52	-12.36	13.39	-4.01	-43.05	10.21	-2.31
	(0.71)	(1.37)	(1.63)	(0.28)	(1.34)	(0.55)	(0.48)
LCITY	38.17	112.56	17.45	106.65	206.04	75.54	56.49
	(1.19)	(1.64)	(0.45)	(1.05)	(0.76)	(0.88)	(1.61)
MCITY	37.45	-76.27	0.29	98.66	490.92	-87.58	13.48
	(1.19)	(1.03)	(0.76)	(0.99)	(1.99)	(0.89)	(0.39)
SCITY	30.96	81.35	-6.86	-13.19	361.09	20.42	14.20
	(1.08)	(1.33)	(0.20)	(0.14)	(1.52)	(0.26)	(0.46)
SUBCITY	20.93	-8.83	-3.43	34.95	93.37	112.90	26.63
	(0.65)	(0.12)	(0.09)	(0.34)	(0.34)	(0.34)	(0.73)
BACKGIVE	2.52	-37.55	10.37	-53.88	234.66	22.47	-24.92
	(0.12)	(0.77)	(0.37)	(0.79)	(1.37)	(0.37)	(1.02)
BACKREL	0.64	-4.30	-23.44	50.68	-31.32	-41.79	3.19
	(0.03)	(0.10)	(0.94)	(0.82)	(0.25)	(0.74)	(0.14)
BACKED	-0.12	-36.54	7.93	44.25	23.30	-34.43	2.23
	(0.01)	(0.88)	(0.32)	(0.77)	(0.21)	(0.61)	(0.10)
HELPER	0.001	0.07	0.004	-0.12	0.33	0.007	
	(0.01)	(0.66)	(0.06)	(0.59)	(1.02)	(0.05)	
YGKID	3.79	40.03	-26.76	100.71	164.26	-185.77	-49.97
	(0.17)	(0.80)	(0.87)	(1.46)	(1.15)	(2.35)	(1.92)
OTHKID	32.27	-2.17	64.32	175.53	-91.45	27.73	-1.68
	(1.76)	(0.51)	(2.56)	(2.82)	(0.72)	(0.45)	(0.08)
YRNBH	0.36	0.81	0.21	3.51	7.02	2.22	0.38
	(0.58)	(0.54)	(0.26)	(1.70)	(1.79)	(1.35)	(0.50)
EDUC	-2.66	39.47	6.67	63.02	79.36	41.34	2.57
	(0.42)	(2.74)	(3.00)	(0.81)	(1.85)	(2.26)	(0.35)
WHITE	60.23	-68.83	-2.28	158.83	290.40	-32.15	63.64
	(1.88)	(1.13)	(0.06)	(1.44)	(1.18)	(0.44)	(1.98)
AGE	2.79	26.82	0.42	44.27	16.45	-7.77	-0.47
	(0.54)	(2.02)	(0.06)	(2.05)	(0.46)	(0.51)	(0.11)
AGE^2	0.03	-0.31	0.004	-0.55	-0.25	0.03	-0.02
	(0.54)	(2.06)	(0.63)	(2.16)	(0.62)	(0.20)	(0.36)
PERPOOR	-1.72	-7.36	0.014	-5.18	-6.86	-2.97	-1.55
	(1.00)	(1.82)	(0.01)	(0.91)	(0.54)	(0.60)	(0.87)
PCINC	-16.67	-94.51	-23.35	30.10	79.32	-47.18	-19.16
	(0.87)	(1.97)	(0.81)	(0.39)	(0.66)	(0.75)	(0.88)

Table A7.2 (continued)

Independent Variables	Fund-raising	Leadership	Clerical/Manual	Teaching	Professional	Counseling	Helper
FEMALE	23.57 (1.13)	-99.47 (1.77)	59.50 (2.01)	2.23 (0.03)	-32.81 (0.22)	69.47 (1.20)	22.65 (0.88)
MARRIED	-16.60 (0.74)	68.32 (1.19)	11.47 (0.36)	-68.75 (0.87)	-75.69 (0.48)	0.13 (0.01)	81.34 (2.98)
OTHGIV	0.20 (0.32)	0.45 (0.35)	-1.51 (1.64)	2.94 (1.44)	9.04 (2.34)	-0.87 (0.45)	0.23 (0.32)
STATEGOV	0.13 (1.26)						
WELFARE		-1.57 (1.70)	-0.66 (1.32)			-1.17 (1.04)	-0.95 (2.19)
CASH		3.23 (2.04)	1.80 (2.09)			2.14 (1.10)	1.46 (2.04)
HIED				1.10 (1.30)			
LOWED				-2.05 (1.78)			
HOSP					1.81 (0.68)		
HEALTH					-22.12 (2.30)		
LOCGOV	0.29 (1.56)			0.09 (0.17)	0.43 (0.44)		
LOCSW		-2.81 (1.77)	-0.81 (1.00)			-0.11 (0.07)	0.008 (1.18)
CONSTANT	-53.52 (0.28)	-62.34 (0.13)	-131.34 (0.52)	-1988.86 (2.85)	-3059.59 (2.35)	-1.63 (0.01)	3.25 (1.53)
1/s	.009	.004	.006	.003	.002	.004	.004

Note: the number of observations for each equation is 734. ·

[a]T-statistics in parentheses.

Table A7.3
Donations of Time by Type of Volunteer Activity[a]: Tobit Regression Results[b]

Independent Variables	Equation				
	Leadership	Clerical/ Manual	Counseling	Professional	Helper
PRICE	-461.10	-4.83	-22.07	60.29	-69.51
	(2.45)	(0.05)	(0.10)	(0.11)	(0.82)
INCOME	0.002	-0.003	-0.003	-.008	-0.001
	(0.94)	(1.56)	(0.69)	(1.41)	(0.22)
NETWAGE	-12.59	13.32	9.78	-41.03	-1.70
	(1.38)	(1.66)	(0.52)	(1.29)	(0.36)
LCITY	105.95	11.72	60.92	234.40	54.22
	(1.51)	(0.29)	(0.69)	(0.87)	(1.50)
MCITY	-74.81	-0.007	-88.21	502.47	16.52
	(1.00)	(0.01)	(0.89)	(2.03)	(0.48)
SCITY	77.80	-3.75	24.93	361.44	10.54
	(1.26)	(0.11)	(0.32)	(1.52)	(0.34)
SUBCITY	-14.02	-12.48	-128.03	121.48	18.54
	(0.20)	(0.30)	(1.23)	(0.45)	(0.51)
BACKGIVE	-47.94	9.93	-23.52	236.23	-33.37
	(0.99)	(0.36)	(0.38)	(1.41)	(1.38)
BACKREL	-0.56	-20.05	-38.12	-42.04	4.19
	(0.01)	(0.83)	(0.67)	(0.34)	(0.19)
BACKED	-22.45	9.05	-27.17	4.58	3.63
	(0.54)	(0.36)	(0.49)	(0.04)	(0.17)
HELPER	0.10	0.02	-0.03	0.32	
	(0.90)	(0.28)	(0.22)	(1.03)	
YGKID	42.23	-27.31	-185.94	166.42	-56.25
	(0.83)	(0.87)	(2.32)	(1.17)	(2.12)
OTHKID	1.02	65.98	27.93	-99.02	4.04
	(0.06)	(2.59)	(0.46)	(0.78)	(0.18)
YRNBH	0.71	0.13	2.26	7.13	0.33
	(0.47)	(0.17)	(1.37)	(1.81)	(0.43)
EDUC	42.28	7.68	42.08	67.98	1.63
	(2.90)	(0.93)	(2.29)	(1.61)	(0.22)
WHITE	-83.83	-4.60	-26.98	330.16	38.67
	(1.36)	(0.13)	(0.36)	(1.30)	(1.17)
AGE	26.81	-0.56	-8.71	25.93	-8.54
	(2.00)	(0.08)	(0.56)	(0.71)	(1.51)
AGE^2	-0.31	0.02	0.04	-0.37	-0.07
	(2.05)	(0.20)	(0.25)	(0.88)	(1.10)
PERPOOR	-8.39	-0.09	-3.20	-4.68	-2.97
	(2.08)	(0.04)	(0.67)	(0.38)	(1.56)
PCINC	-57.81	-14.60	-49.22	110.73	-17.48
	(1.29)	(0.53)	(0.83)	(0.89)	(0.75)

Table A7.3 (continued)

Independent Variables	Equation				
	Leadership	Clerical/ Manual	Counseling	Professional	Helper
FEMALE	-94.19	57.83	71.90	-61.78	20.12
	(1.67)	(1.96)	(1.25)	(0.42)	(0.79)
MARRIED	62.05	7.35	-4.28	-110.45	69.60
	(1.07)	(0.23)	(0.07)	(0.70)	(2.55)
OTHGIV	0.28	-1.77	-0.82	7.44	0.36
	(0.20)	(1.82)	(0.40)	(1.95)	(0.47)
STATEGOV	-0.11	0.18	0.008	-0.53	0.09
	(0.42)	(1.17)	(0.02)	(0.80)	(0.66)
LOCGOV	-0.27	0.08	0.32	0.29	-0.42
	(0.60)	(0.28)	(0.55)	(0.24)	(1.85)
CONSTANT	150.44	-230.28	60.09	-3190.33	325.49
	(0.32)	(0.43)	(0.11)	(2.44)	(1.54)
1/s	.004	.006	.004	.002	.004

Note: the number of observations for each equation is 734.

[a]With aggregate state and local government spending replacing disaggregated measures in Table A7.2.

[b]T-statistics in parentheses.

8.

Giving and Government: Time Series Analysis

INTRODUCTION

I turn now to re-examine the relationship between charitable giving and government spending in a manner different from, but complementary to, that in Chapters 6 and 7. Rather than analyzing survey data for individuals in a given year, this chapter looks at the historical relationship between aggregate national giving and various measures of government spending for the years 1930 through 1986.

What Can Time-Series Analysis Tell Us?

The time-series approach of this chapter provides valuable additional information on a number of issues. First, it provides evidence about whether the relationship between government spending and charitable giving has changed over time. This relationship may, for instance, have changed in the mid-1960s, with the advent of the War on Poverty. On the one hand, the rapid rise in government social welfare spending may have increased the extent to which crowding out took place. On the other hand, with the War on Poverty also came a new, closer relationship between government and the nonprofit sector, with more and more government-financed activities being carried out by private nonprofit organizations. As was noted in previous chapters, changes in government support to charities may have very different effects on giving than do changes in other types of spending, such as cash transfers directly to the poor.

This issue is investigated by estimating separate models for different time periods within the years 1930 to 1986. We can then examine the estimated relationship between giving and government spending for these different periods and formally test whether or not these relationships have, in fact, changed.

In addition, this approach will provide information regarding the relevance of the estimates in Chapters 6 and 7, which are based on a 1974 survey, for the current world. The issue here is not whether government spending or charitable giving have changed significantly since 1974—for surely they have—but whether the relationship between the two (or between giving and other key variables) has changed. We address this issue by examining whether a model estimated for the post–War on Poverty years, 1965 to 1986, predicts giving as well for the 1980s as it does for the 1960s and 1970s.

One interesting aspect of this question is whether President Reagan and others were successful in increasing national giving in the face of reduced government social welfare spending, via exhortations and "moral suasion," beyond what it would otherwise have been. That is, was actual charitable giving during the Reagan years greater than would be predicted by our model?

Finally, the analysis of time-series data can tell us about the importance of lags in donor behavior. We can examine whether charitable giving is influenced by current government spending, past spending, or perhaps both. It may be that donor response to changes in government behavior take place only gradually.

Shortcomings of the Data

Despite the value of time-series analysis, the data do have some important limitations that should be kept in mind when interpreting results. First, historical data are available only for aggregate charitable giving and not for giving to particular types of charity, such as religious, health-related, or educational organizations. I argued in Chapter 6 that this aggregation of different types of giving was an important shortcoming of previous analyses of charitable giving.

Because the giving is not disaggregated, it is not possible to match giving in a particular area with government spending in that area, as was done with the survey data. In the analysis, therefore, giving is assumed to depend on a single measure of total spending by federal, state, and local governments or, alternatively, on federal and state/local social welfare spending.

Since the giving data comes from two separate sources, they may present problems. Ralph Nelson has estimated giving by living donors from 1929 through 1970.[1] Giving for the years 1955 to 1986 has been independently estimated by the American Association of Fundraising Counsel in its annual report, *Giving USA*. Because these two series give slightly different estimates for the years of overlap, it was necessary to "splice" them together, by estimating a relationship between the two series for the years in common and using that relationship to adjust the estimates for 1929 through 1955.

In addition, many of the variables included in the analysis of the survey of giving are unavailable in the time-series context. For instance, while the survey data allowed us to control, albeit imperfectly, for differences in attitudes across individuals, it is impossible to control for changes in attitudes over time in the same manner. The time-series analysis does control for changes in personal income, as well as the size and median age of the population. However, if other unobserved variables that influence giving have changed historically and are correlated with the included variables, then coefficient estimates may be biased.

Finally, no time-series data on volunteering are available. The discussion in this chapter is, therefore, limited to contributions of money.

GIVING AND GOVERNMENT SPENDING, 1930–1986

I begin by estimating, by ordinary least squares regression, several, alternative models of charitable giving for the entire period of 1930 through 1986 (Appendix, Table A8.1). In the simplest form of this model, aggregate giving is assumed to depend on personal income, population, median age of the population, and total spending by all levels of government.[2] For the period as a whole, total government spending appears to encourage charitable giving. The coefficient for total government spending, TOTGOVT, is significant and suggests that a one dollar rise in TOTGOVT generated, on average, just over two cents in additional giving. Thus, there is no evidence of crowding out at this level of aggregation. Giving also appears to rise with increases in income, population size, and median age, although only the coefficient for income is statistically significant.

The first modification made to this analysis is to consider the possibility that giving responds to changes in government spending only with a lag. I investigate this by including both TOTGOVT and the previous year's (lagged) total government spending, LTOTGOVT. When this addition is made, TOTGOVT no longer affects giving, but LTOTGOVT does; a one dollar increase in government spending in any given year appears to increase giving the following year by approximately 2.3 cents. It seems, then, as though government spending may well affect charitable giving with a lag, at least at the aggregate level.

Social Welfare Spending and Charitable Giving

Because a significant portion of government spending goes toward activities for which the charitable sector provides no close substitute—defense expenditures come to mind—it may be desirable to examine the relationship between giving and the subset of all government expenditures that finances output most similar to that of the charitable sector. Thus, a model was estimated in which government spending includes federal as well as state and local social welfare spending. This includes spending on education, public assistance, other public welfare, health, and hospitals.

For the entire period of 1930 through 1986, the coefficients for both federal welfare spending and state and local welfare spending are significant. The results indicate that federal welfare spending (FEDWELF) crowds out giving, while state and local welfare spending (SLOCWELF) encourages giving. A one dollar increase in FEDWELF reduces giving by a sizable thirty-eight cents, while a dollar rise in SLOCWELF increases donations by just over eight cents.

Within the context of the preceding analysis, this difference between federal and state/local spending would be expected if either the social welfare services provided by federal spending are substitutes for charity while those of states and localities are complements for charity, or if states and localities funnel more of their welfare spending through the private charitable sector.

State and local welfare spending, which includes public assistance programs administered by the states, is far larger than federal welfare spending; state and local spending averaged $69.3 billion annually for the period from 1930 to 1986, while federal spending averaged $11.4 billion. Thus, the larger of the two categories of spending does not crowd out but rather encourages charitable givig. If we imagine both categories of welfare spending growing at an equal rate over time, then the overall effect would be to increase giving. For instance, an additional 10 percent annual growth in all welfare spending over the entire fifty-six years would, other things being equal, have increased giving by approximately $125 million per year, or 0.85 percent, beyond what it, in fact, was.

Income and median age both exert significant positive influence over giving in this model, but increases in population appear, oddly, to reduce giving. This negative coefficient for population may reflect the effect of an omitted variable correlated with population.

Adding lagged federal and state/local welfare spending (LFEDWELF and LSLOCWELF) to the equation has little effect. Neither of the lagged coefficients are significant, and the other coefficients are largely unchanged. Thus, when government spending is disaggregated, the importance of lags disappears, and donors appear to respond to current government spending.

HAVE THE RELATIONSHIPS CHANGED OVER TIME?

I turn next to address the issue of whether or not the relationships between giving and government spending and between giving and the other independent variables, estimated for the entire period 1930 through 1986, were stable over time or whether, instead, grouping the entire fifty-six years together obscures important differences. To address the issue, I estimate separate equations, identical in form to those discussed above, for the years 1930 through 1964 and 1965 through 1986 (Tables A8.4 and A8.5). The year 1964 was chosen because it approximates the beginning of the War on Poverty, which appears to have dramatically altered both expectations regarding the role of government and the relationship between government and the charitable sectors.[3]

Giving and Total Government Spending

It appears from these separate estimates that the relationship between giving and government spending did change substantially between the two time periods. In particular, in the simplest equation estimated with TOTGOVT, the coefficient for government spending is negative and significant for 1930 to 1964, which indicates that government spending historically crowded out charitable giving, at least in the aggregate. A one dollar increase in TOTGOVT reduced giving by .64 cents. This result is in contrast to that for the entire period, 1930 to 1986, in which government spending encouraged giving, as well as for the post-1965 period. For this most recent period, the coefficient is positive and significant, and it implies that a one dollar increase in TOTGOVT increases giving by 2.5 cents. Thus, the result for the entire period from 1930 to 1986, does appear to obscure significant changes over time.

It is difficult, at this level of aggregation, to explain this change convincingly. One possibility, however, is that the mix of goods and services represented by TOTGOVT changed from one that substituted for charity in the pre-1964 period to one that was, in the aggregate, complementary with charitable output. This change could have taken place if either government's output mix or that of the charitable sector changed significantly over time. The latter is broadly consistent with the experience of certain social welfare charities that have attempted to position themselves as complements of government in the face of rapid growth in government's role as a provider of social services. Family Services of America, for instance, shifted from its original role as a provider of goods and services to the needy to one of an advocate or ombudsman for the poor in their dealings with government.[4]

A second possible explanation for the change in the government-charity relationship is that government has come to rely more heavily on private charities to provide services that are publically financed. In the post–War on Poverty era, increases in government spending have come, to a significant degree, in the form of support for private charities. As has been discussed above, such support may well encourage, rather than crowd out, giving.

When lagged total government spending is added to the equation, it has different effects for the two time periods. In the period from 1930 to 1964, LTOTGOVT is insignificant, and its inclusion has little effect on the other coefficients. In the more recent period, however, LTOTGOVT has a significant positive effect, and TOTGOVT is no longer significant. The coefficient of LTOTGOVT implies that one dollar increase in spending in a given year will increase giving the following year by just over three cents. This result is similar to that for the entire period from 1930 to 1986.

The Changing Impact of Social Welfare Spending

Estimated equations including state/local and federal welfare spending also suggest that changes in the relationship between government and giving have taken place over the past five decades. In the period before 1965, each dollar of federal welfare spending led to approximately sixteen cents of increased giving, while a dollar of state and local welfare spending crowded out over fourteen cents of donations. After 1965, however, the direction of these responses to government spending are reversed, and their magnitudes are larger. Now one dollar of federal welfare spending crowds out thirty-one cents in giving, while state and local welfare spending encourages giving, with an eighteen cent rise in donations associated with each additional dollar of state/local welfare spending.

Because state and local welfare spending far exceeded that of the federal government for both periods, these results suggest that the growth of all welfare spending crowded out giving before 1964, but it has increased giving since then. For instance, in the earlier period, an additional 10 percent annual growth in both federal and state/local welfare spending would have led to a fall in giving of approximately $160 million per year, or 3.8 percent of giving for that period. In the post–War on Poverty period, however, an additional annual 10 percent across-the-board growth of welfare spending would lead to an increase in donations of just over $2 billion per year, or 6.5 percent of giving for that period. This is at least consistent with the hypothesized effects, noted at various points throughout this book, of the closer relationship between government and charities that has evolved over the past twenty or so years.

A Formal Test of Stability

Comparing estimated coefficients across the two time periods has led me to infer that the relationship between government spending and charitable giving has changed over time. In this section, a more formal statistical test is conducted of the hypothesis that the coefficients are stable over the two time periods. One can, in effect, test whether splitting the sample into two periods significantly enhances the explanatory power of the model. If it does, then we can reject the hypothesis that the coefficients are equal across the periods.[5]

The results of this test are consistent with the discussion above. For both the equation including TOTGOVT and that including FEDWELF and SLOCWELF, we can reject with 99 percent confidence the hypothesis that the coefficients are equal across time periods. This is true whether the cutoff year is 1964 or 1974.[6] Thus, there have been structural changes in the model over time.

ARE THE SURVEY ESTIMATES STILL RELEVANT?

I argued in Chapter 6 that the *National Survey of Philanthropy* was the best available data source for addressing the concerns of this book. Nevertheless, the fact that the survey was conducted in 1974 suggests that the results should be interpreted with care.

In this section, I use the time-series data to address the applicability of results from the survey to giving in the 1980s and beyond. One approach would be to split the years from 1974 to 1986 into two time periods and compare coefficients, or to test formally the hypothesis that coefficients are equal across periods. This approach, however, is not feasible here given the small sample size (six observations per period) that would result. Therefore, I take a less formal tack. I examine the data and regression results from 1965 to 1986 to see whether actual levels of giving are predicted as well, using these data, for the 1980s as for the 1960s and 1970s. If they are, this would offer at least tentative support for the claim that the survey results, reported in Chapters 6 and 7, are still useful for understanding giving behavior.

Actual and Predicted Giving with the TOTGOVT Equation

For 1965 to 1986 we can see that the extent to which giving is mispredicted varies from a low of 0.57 percent in 1978 to a high of 9.3 percent in 1972 (Table 8.1). More important is the fact that the performance of the model is just as good, if not better, in the most recent years of the period as in the earlier years. The average percentage prediction error for the period 1965 to 1974 is 4.7 percent, compared with only 2.1 percent for 1975 to 1986.

It appears, then, that giving in the mid-1980s is not particularly unusual from the perspective of the entire post-1965 period; data from the 1960s through the 1980s predicts giving in the mid-1980s quite well. This accuracy should increase confidence in the *National Survey of Philanthropy* as a data source on which to quantify and understand current and future giving.

A second way of addressing the issue of whether giving in the 1980s is systematically different from giving in the recent past is to examine whether or not giving in the 1980s is systematically under- or over-predicted by the model. Even if the size of our prediction error is small for recent years, if it is consistently in one direction, then one might infer that something is different about those years. It is true that giving is under-predicted for

Table 8.1
Actual and Predicted Giving, 1965–1986, Using Total Government Spending as an Explanatory Variable[a]

Year	Actual Giving	Predicted Giving	Residual[b]	Residual as % of Actual Giving
1965	10.00	9.73	0.27	2.60
1966	10.60	10.68	-0.08	0.74
1967	11.30	11.80	-0.50	4.44
1968	12.50	12.90	-0.40	3.17
1969	13.30	14.04	-0.74	5.58
1970	14.00	14.88	-0.88	6.29
1971	17.60	16.29	1.30	7.42
1972	19.40	17.60	1.80	9.30
1973	20.50	19.41	1.09	5.32
1974	21.60	21.15	0.45	2.09
1975	23.50	23.98	-0.48	2.06
1976	26.30	26.64	-0.34	1.31
1977	29.60	29.14	0.46	1.55
1978	32.10	32.28	-0.18	0.57
1979	36.60	36.18	0.42	1.15
1980	40.70	41.28	-0.58	1.42
1981	46.40	47.18	-0.78	1.68
1982	48.50	51.30	-2.80	5.77
1983	53.50	55.54	-2.04	3.80
1984	60.70	59.63	1.07	1.76
1985	66.10	65.18	0.92	1.39
1986	71.70	69.67	2.03	2.83

[a]From OLS regression, 1965-86, including TOTGOVT as an explanatory variable.

[b]Actual Giving minus Predicted Giving.

each of the last three years examined here. However, for the first four years of the 1980s, giving was over-predicted. Thus, there is no obvious systematic bias, although such a bias could conceivably become apparent when data on giving through the 1980s becomes available.

The fact that actual giving was less in the early 1980s than our model would predict—and a good deal less in 1982 and 1983—casts doubt on the notion that the Reagan administration was successful at stimulating giving through moral suasion. There is no strong evidence of a "Reagan effect."

Table 8.2
Actual and Predicted Giving, 1965–1986, Using Federal and State/Local Welfare Spending as Explanatory Variables[a]

Year	Actual Giving	Predicted Giving	Residual[b]	Residual as % of Actual Giving
1965	10.00	9.92	0.08	0.81
1966	10.60	10.67	-0.07	0.66
1967	11.30	11.13	0.17	1.49
1968	12.50	12.26	0.24	1.91
1969	13.30	13.47	-0.17	1.28
1970	14.00	15.08	-1.08	7.70
1971	17.60	16.97	0.63	3.59
1972	19.40	18.86	0.54	2.79
1973	20.50	20.83	-0.32	1.60
1974	21.60	21.96	-0.36	1.67
1975	23.50	23.43	0.07	0.30
1976	26.30	26.03	0.27	1.03
1977	29.60	29.18	0.42	1.41
1978	32.10	32.63	-0.53	1.66
1979	36.60	35.84	0.76	2.08
1980	40.70	40.85	-0.15	0.36
1981	46.40	46.11	0.29	0.63
1982	48.50	50.23	-1.73	3.56
1983	53.50	53.47	0.03	0.06
1984	60.70	60.05	0.65	1.07
1985	66.10	65.55	0.55	0.83
1986	71.70	71.98	-0.28	0.40

[a]From OLS regression, 1965-86, including SLOCWELF and FEDWELF as explanatory variables.

[b]Actual Giving minus Predicted Giving.

Predicting Giving with FEDWELF and SLOCWELF

The results of the analysis for equations including social welfare spending are presented in Table 8.2. Prediction errors are considerably smaller here than in the TOTGOVT model: errors range from .06 percent in 1983 to 7.7 percent in 1970.

Again, this model predicts giving more closely in recent years. The average prediction error for the period from 1965 to 1974 was 2.35 percent, compared with only 1.12 percent for 1975 to 1986. Giving in the 1980s is predicted particularly well, with an average error of under 1 percent. Thus, there is again no reason to believe that the relationships estimated with data from 1965 through 1986 have dramatically changed in the 1980s.

There also appears to have been no systematic bias in the predictions for the 1980s. In three years of the 1980s, actual giving was less than predicted, and in the other four actual giving exceeded predicted giving. There is again no evidence of a Reagan effect.

NOTES

1. See Bureau of the Census, U.S. Department of Commerce, *Historical Statistics of the United States, Colonial Times to 1970, Part 1: Social Statistics*, Series H-399.

2. Complete regression results, as well as means and variances of variables, are presented in the Appendix to this chapter.

3. The data were also split at 1974 to test for the sensitivity of our results to the choice of cutoff dates. See Tables A8.2 and A8.3 in the Appendix to this chapter for those regression results.

4. This example is discussed by Rose-Ackerman (1981).

5. The test for stability is an F-test. The test statistic is:

$$\frac{(RRSS - URSS)/(k+1)}{URSS/(n_1 + n_2 - 2k - 2)}$$

where RRSS is the restricted residual sum of squares, obtained from the regression utilizing all years from 1930 to 1986. The value *URSS* is the unrestricted residual sum of squares, the sum of the residual sum of squares from the two separate equations. The number of observations in the two time periods are n_1 and n_2, and the number of coefficients, including the constant, is $k + 1$. The test statistic is distributed $F(k + 1, n_1 + n_2 - 2k - 2)$.

6. The value of the test statistic with the cutoff at 1964 is 3.61 in the TOTGOVT equation, and 9.95 in the equation with FEDWELF and SLOCWELF. With the cutoff at 1974, the values are 14.19 and 5.92.

Appendix

Table A8.1
Charitable Donations of Money, 1930–1986: OLS Time Series Analysis[a]

Independent Variable	Equation			
	1	2	3	4
INCOME	0.009** (3.39)	0.010** (3.63)	0.019** (9.74)	0.019** (9.22)
POPULATION	0.007 (0.88)	0.005 (0.73)	-0.031** (6.46)	-0.033** (5.74)
MEDIAN AGE	0.127 (1.03)	0.111 (1.00)	0.416** (3.85)	0.416** (3.81)
TOTGOVT	0.022** (4.29)	-0.001 (0.16)		
LTOTGOVT		0.023** (3.63)		
FEDWELF			-0.377** (9.51)	-0.397** (4.99)
LFEDWELF				0.0204 (0.22)
SLCOWELF			0.083** (3.90)	0.125** (2.36)
LSLOCWELF				-0.049 (0.88)
CONSTANT	-4.48 (1.19)	-3.84 (1.13)	-7.97** (2.46)	-7.82** (2.38)
R^2	.99769	.99818	.99889	.99891

Note: the number of observations for these equations is 56.

[a]T-statistics in parentheses.

*Coefficient significant at .10 or better.

**Coefficient significant at .01 or better.

Table A8.2
Charitable Donations of Money, 1930–1973: OLS Time Series Analysis[a]

Independent Variable	Equation			
	1	2	3	4
INCOME	0.022** (8.67)	0.022** (8.11)	0.005 (1.14)	0.005 (1.15)
POPULATION	-0.004 (0.43)	-0.004 (0.42)	0.037** (2.35)	0.042** (2.55)
MEDIAN AGE	0.188** (2.69)	0.188** (2.64)	0.400** (4.12)	0.369** (3.56)
TOTGOVT	-0.008 (1.45)	-0.008 (1.23)		
LTOTGOVT		0.001 (0.05)		
FEDWELF			-0.057 (0.58)	-0.034 (0.22)
LFEDWELF				0.081 (0.58)
SLCOWELF			0.109** (3.17)	0.010 (0.12)
LSLOCWELF				0.099 (1.15)
CONSTANT	-5.19** (2.63)	-5.17 (2.57)	-15.57** (4.02)	-15.35** (3.76)
R^2	.99286	.99642	.99410	.99450

Note: the number of observations for these equations is 43.

[a]T-statistics in parentheses·

*Coefficient significant at .10 or better.

**Coefficient significant at .01 or better.

Table A8.3
Charitable Donations of Money, 1974–1986: OLS Time Series Analysis[a]

Independent Variable	Equation			
	1	2	3	4
INCOME	0.025** (2.87)	0.026** (2.87)	0.018** (3.78)	0.016 (1.42)
POPULATION	-1.778** (3.23)	-1.600** (2.59)	-1.290 (1.44)	-1.040 (0.76)
MEDIAN AGE	5.700* (1.93)	3.890 (0.99)	3.400 (1.18)	3.880 (1.06)
TOTGOVT	0.019** (2.27)	0.007 (0.36)		
LTOTGOVT		0.011 (0.73)		
FEDWELF			-0.125 (0.69)	-0.173 (0.72)
LFEDWELF				-0.004 (0.02)
SLCOWELF			-0.168** (3.78)	0.209* (1.98)
LSLOCWELF				-0.051 (0.44)
CONSTANT	200.01* (1.77)	213.66* (1.81)	161.35 (1.15)	98.02 (0.41)
R^2	.99758	.99775	.99873	.99875

Note: the number of observations for these regressions is 13.

[a]T-statistics in parentheses.

*Coefficient significant at .10 or better

**Coefficient significant at .01 or better

Table A8.4
Charitable Donations of Money, 1930–1964: OLS Time Series Analysis[a]

Independent Variable	Equation 1	2	3	4
INCOME	0.019** (4.33)	0.019** (4.23)	0.015** (4.52)	0.017** (5.45)
POPULATION	0.023 (0.90)	0.022 (0.87)	0.101** (3.08)	0.086** (2.82)
MEDIAN AGE	0.103** (2.41)	0.103** (2.38)	-0.210* (1.87)	-0.234** (2.27)
TOTGOVT	-0.006** (2.23)	-0.006* (1.76)		
LTOTGOVT		0.001 (0.26)		
FEDWELF			0.157** (2.84)	-0.048 (0.44)
LFEDWELF				0.243** (2.63)
SLCOWELF			-0.144** (2.67)	-0.056 (0.55)
LSLOCWELF				-0.092 (0.99)
CONSTANT	-5.95* (1.73)	-5.90* (1.69)	-6.70** (2.20)	-4.21 (1.43)
R^2	.99414	.99416	.99542	.99648

Note: the number of observations for these equations is 34.

[a]T-statistics in parentheses.

*Coefficient significant at .10 or better.

**Coefficient significant at .01 or better.

Table A8.5
Charitable Donations of Money, 1965–1986: OLS Time Series Analysis

Independent Variable	Equation			
	1	2	3	4
INCOME	0.009 (1.18)	0.015** (2.05)	0.012** (3.94)	0.013** (3.80)
POPULATION	-0.053 (0.48)	-0.034 (0.34)	-0.277** (2.85)	0.260** (2.39)
MEDIAN AGE	-0.673 (0.31)	-1.960 (0.98)	0.175 (0.15)	0.615 (0.41)
TOTGOVT	0.025** (2.41)	-0.011 (0.60)		
LTOTGOVT		0.031** (2.35)		
FEDWELF			-0.312** (5.21)	-0.296** (2.58)
LFEDWELF				-0.045 (0.40)
SLCOWELF			0.181** (4.94)	0.201** (2.78)
LSLOCWELF				-0.030 (0.38)
CONSTANT	28.69 (0.45)	59.11 (1.01)	45.94 (1.18)	30.47 (0.59)
R^2	.99638	.99731	.99907	.99910

Note: the number of observations for these equations is 22.

*Coefficient significant at .10 or better

**Coefficient significant at .01 or better

Table A8.6
Means and Standard Deviations for Time-Series Variables, Various
Time Periods

Variable	Time Period			
	1930-86		1930-73	
	Mean	Std.Dev.	Mean	Std.Dev.
Giving[1]	14.73	18.01	6.22	7.01
Median Age	29.18	1.21	28.89	1.18
Personal Income	790.62	973.54	339.24	277.22
Population[2]	176.80	38.17	161.44	29.06
Total Government Spending[1]	336.83	436.25	129.84	113.62
Lagged[1]	306.72	397.16	119.92	104.43
Federal Welfare Spending[1]	11.36	16.75	2.88	3.38
Lagged[1]	10.39	15.75	2.56	2.98
State Welfare Spending[1]	69.29	91.82	24.56	27.80
Lagged[1]	63.28	84.49	22.15	24.80

[1]Billions of dollars

[2]Millions

Table A8.6 (continued)

	Time Period			
	1974-86		1930-64	
Variable	Mean	Std.Dev.	Mean	Std.Dev.
Giving[1]	42.87	16.54	4.07	2.87
Median Age	30.15	1.02	29.13	1.15
Personal Income	2283.66	784.02	220.61	142.97
Population[2]	227.58	9.18	159.43	21.65
Total Government Spending[1]	1021.47	407.15	81.35	57.86
Lagged	924.61	382.30	75.87	55.40
Federal Welfare Spending[1]	39.45	11.53	1.40	1.10
Lagged	36.29	12.65	1.36	1.07
State Welfare Spending[1]	217.23	71.11	12.32	10.46
Lagged	199.30	66.78	11.34	9.60

[1]Billions of dollars

[2]Millions

Table A8.6 (continued)

Variable	Time Period 1965-86 Mean	Std.Dev.
Giving[1]	31.21	19.18
Median Age	29.26	1.34
Personal Income	1671.55	964.86
Population[2]	217.55	14.64
Total Government Spending[1]	731.66	473.48
Lagged	663.50	434.35
Federal Welfare Spending[1]	26.76	18.01
Lagged	24.43	17.55
State Welfare Spending[1]	157.33	92.38
Lagged	143.55	86.21

[1]Billions of dollars

2Millions

9.

Charitable Giving: The 1980s and Beyond

INTRODUCTION

The previous eight chapters have presented a theoretical and empirical analysis of charitable giving, with particular emphasis on the impact of government policies on donations of both money and time. This chapter uses this analysis to evaluate the influence on the charitable sector of two major economic developments of the 1980s—tax reform and the reduction in the growth of government social welfare spending—and to hypothesize about the future of giving in America.

The charitable sector has experienced profound changes over the past decade. A reduction in government's role as a provider of social services has increased pressure on the charitable sector to "fill the gap" just as other changes—particularly cuts in government support for charities and tax reform—have made it more difficult for charitable organizations to raise needed revenue. The ways in which charities and donors have responded to these changes is the subject addressed here.

TAX POLICY AND GIVING IN THE 1980s

Table 9.1 indicates that the price of giving has risen for the typical donor by approximately 11 percent in the 1980s—a substantial rise. If, for example, the price elasticity of giving is 1.25,[1] then the result of the price increase has been to reduce money donations by approximately 14 percent, or $11 billion, compared to what they would otherwise have been.

In order to understand the causes of this overall price increase, it is useful to divide the decade into three periods. In the first period, 1980 to 1984, there were largely offsetting pressures on the price of giving. On the one hand, the tax cuts of 1981, by reducing the value of the charitable deduction, increased the price of a money donation for itemizers. At the same time, however, the percentage of taxpayers itemizing increased from 30.9 percent in 1980 to 38.2 percent in 1984.[2] Thus, while the implicit subsidy of charitable giving fell per itemizer, there were by 1984 more individuals receiving at least some subsidy. The years 1982 to 1984 were also the first years of the phase-in of the charitable deduction for non-itemizers. As can be seen in Table 9.1, however, this provision was initially of little value.[3] The overall effect of these changes was to slightly increase the price of giving.

The second period, from 1984 to 1986, is characterized by a fairly rapid decline in the price of a money donation. Over this period, the phase-in of the "above-the-line" deduction for non-itemizers was completed, bringing about a large reduction in the cost of giving for these donors. In addition, the proportion of taxpayers itemizing continued to rise.

The third, and most damaging, period began with the Tax Reform Act of 1986 and continues to the present. Tax reform increases the price of giving for itemizers by lowering marginal tax rates. In addition, the elimination of many deductions will undoubtedly reduce the number of itemizers, thereby limiting the number of donors who receive any subsidy. Finally, the repeal of the above-the-line deduction eliminates the subsidy to donors who do not itemize.

Table 9.1
Average Price of a Money Donation, Itemizers and Nonitemizers, 1980–1988

| Year | Type of Taxpayer | | |
	Itemizers	Non-Itemizers	All
1980	0.685	1.00	0.740
1981	0.686	1.00	0.743
1982	0.702	0.998	0.756
1983	0.711	0.998	0.763
1984	0.715	0.990	0.764
1985	0.717	0.823	0.736
1986	0.718	0.681	0.710
1987	0.746	1.00	0.791
1988	0.780	1.00	0.820

Source: Calculations were made by Lawrence Lindsey, using the National Bureau of Economic Research tax simulation model.

[a]The price represents a weighted average, with weights based on the amounts of charitable giving by income groups.

TAX REFORM AND THE CHARITABLE SECTOR

Much concern has been voiced that tax reform will, for these reasons, have a disastrous effect on charitable giving and, thus, on the ability of the sector to provide goods and services. For instance, Lindsey (1987) estimates that the 1986 tax act will reduce giving by between 14.2 and 17.7 percent per year, compared with what it would have been in the absence of tax reform.

Predictions of this sort are made by first calculating the effect of the tax changes on the price of giving for individuals in different income groups and then applying estimated price elasticities of giving to these price changes.[4] While such predictions provide valuable information for policy analysis, they tell only part of the story. Tax reform will affect the charitable sector in ways that are much more far reaching than simply reducing donations of money by individuals. Some of these effects will exacerbate the predicted negative impact of tax reform on contributions of money, while others will offset it.

Tax Reform and Volunteering

Volunteering is an extremely valuable resource to charitable organizations. In fact, it is approximately as important as money donations (see Chapter 5). Tax reform is likely to have a strong negative impact on hours volunteered, so that charitable organizations will tend to find it more difficult to raise contributions of both money and time.

First, tax reform will discourage volunteering via a direct price effect. Recall that the price of volunteering for an individual is his or her net-of-tax wage rate. Thus, the lower marginal tax rates brought about by the Tax Reform Act of 1986 will, by making working for pay more attractive relative to volunteering, reduce hours donated.

In addition, tax reform will influence giving through its impact on the price of a money donation—the cross-price effect. The results of Chapter 7 indicate that money and time donations are complements, so that a rise in the price of giving money will reduce donations of both money and time.[5]

There has not been enough research done on the economics of volunteering to predict with great confidence the impact of changes in tax policy on volunteering. However, utilizing the analysis presented in Chapter 7 as well as that of Menchik and Weisbrod (1987), I have estimated that the 1986 tax reform will reduce hours volunteered by between 6 and 20 percent.[6] Thus, simulations that focus on donations of money only may seriously understate tax reform's impact on the charitable sector.

Corporations and Foundations

While I have focused on contributions by individuals, over 10 percent of all money donations come from corporations and foundations.[7] Relatively little is known about the determinants of giving by these organizations. However, it is likely that tax reform, by reducing the top corporate tax rate from 46 to 34 percent while, at the same time increasing the overall corporate tax burden, will lead to a decline in corporate donations. Clotfelter (1987) estimates that this decline will be on the order of 5 percent of corporate giving.

On the other hand, it is at least plausible that corporations and foundations will respond to any reductions in giving by individuals by raising their own giving. This view is supported by anecdotal evidence that corporations increased and redirected their giving to benefit those types of organizations hardest hit by Reagan administration budget cuts.[8]

Responses by Charities

Until now I have focused on donor responses to tax law changes. However, the charitable organizations themselves may respond to lost revenues in ways that soften the blow of tax reform. They may, for instance, increase their solicitations. A recent *New York Times* article,[9] for instance, noted that "Nonprofit theatres have developed sophisticated fund-raising strategies in response to escalating operating costs, changing tax laws and uncertain economic conditions." To the extent that charitable organizations can increase donations by increased solicitations and improved strategies for fund-raising, the Tax Reform Act of 1986 may have a less drastic impact on charitable giving. However, only the increase in giving net of solicitations can be considered a true gain to the sector, since only those net revenues are available for providing goods and services.

In addition to increasing solicitations, charities may pursue new sources of revenue, such as user fees. While such a response could enable a charity to maintain its overall size, it would not be without its negative effects. The often needy clients of these charitable organizations would now be forced to pay for at least some portion of the cost of services provided to them, previously financed by donations.

Charities may also turn to commercial sales to offset losses in more preferred sources of revenue, such as donations. Hospitals, for instance, may operate laundry services or museums may increase their gift shop sales. As in the case of increased soliciting, however, it is only the net profits, and not the total sales revenue, from commercial sales that are available for the provision of charitable goods and services. In addition, the pursuit of commercial profits may itself reduce donations and could conceivably subvert the primary purpose of the charitable organization.

Schiff and Weisbrod (1987) find that social welfare charities do, in fact, respond to losses in preferred revenue sources by turning to user fees and commercial sales. For instance, we estimate that a dollar decline in vendor payments[10] from government to the charitable sector results in an increase of almost ninety cents in sales revenue. Thus charities do appear to have an ability to respond to external changes in creative ways, although the consequences of such changes may not always be socially desirable.

Finally, it is possible that, facing reduced revenues, charitable organizations will operate more efficiently, by reducing waste. A predominant view among economists holds that because nonprofit managers cannot appropriate profits, they have little incentive to behave in a cost-effective manner.[11] If there is any truth to this, there is room for potential cost reductions without cuts in service levels, and losses in contributions may not have as drastic an effect as expected on the provision of charitable services.

The Reshaping of the Charitable Sector

The Tax Reform Act of 1986 will have a dramatic impact on the charitable sector. As others have noted, money donations by individuals will grow very slowly, although the impact on contributions may be less than expected if charities step up their fund-raising efforts. It is likely that volunteering will also fall, and the best estimate is that it will do so by about 10 percent per year.

Thus, charities will be forced to make do with less charitable giving.[12] As a result, some charities will exit, leaving less variety for donors. In addition, we will likely see the surviving charities engaged in a wider variety of activities and relying on a correspondingly broader range of revenue sources. The challenge facing charitable organizations is to pursue these alternative revenue sources without losing track of their primary, charitable purpose.

CHARITIES AND THE RETRENCHMENT OF GOVERNMENT

The 1980s have seen a sharp reversal in the trend, evident through the 1960s and 1970s, of increased government spending on social welfare. As indicated in Table 9.2, social welfare spending by all levels of government (Public Aid plus Other Welfare) has failed to keep pace with inflation. In particular, those types of government spending that are channeled through the charitable sector—"Other Welfare"—have fallen sharply.

As illustrated in Table 9.3, support from government to social service nonprofits fell by over 11 percent in the first term of the Reagan administration. This figure is particularly discouraging given the increased expectations placed on the charitable sector as a direct result of cuts in social welfare spending in general.

Did Crowding Out Take Place?

The response of donors to the reduced role for government is, as discussed at great length, quite complex. On the one hand, cutbacks in service provision should induce extra giving by individuals—i.e., crowding out should occur. On the other hand, the reduction in government support for the sector makes giving money less attractive, while making volunteering more so.

What has been the overall impact of government cutbacks on charitable giving in the 1980s? Private donations of money to social welfare organizations rose, after inflation, by about $1 billion, or 27 percent between 1980 and 1984. It is difficult to separate out the impact of the changes in government spending from other changes taking place at the same time. However, a "back-of-the-envelope" calculation is instructive. Over the period from 1980 to 1984, the average price of giving rose by 3.2 percent (see Table 9.1). This alone would reduce giving by somewhere on the

Table 9.2
Selected Social Welfare Spending Under Public Programs, 1977–1985[a]:
Current and Inflation-Adjusted (1977) Dollars

Year	Public Aid[b] Current Dollars	Public Aid[b] 1977 Dollars	Other Welfare[c] Current Dollars	Other Welfare[c] 1977 Dollars
1977	53.3	53.3	9.1	9.1
1978	59.4	55.2	10.6	9.8
1979	64.7	53.4	11.1	9.2
1980	71.8	52.8	13.6	10.0
1981	82.4	54.9	12.0	8.0
1982	80.9	50.8	11.7	7.3
1983	85.8	52.2	12.5	7.6
1984	89.9	52.4	13.5	7.8
1985	96.0	54.0	13.9	7.8
% Change 1977-85	80.1	1.3	52.7	-13.6
% Change 1980-85	33.7	2.3	2.0	-22.0

Source: *Social Security Bulletin*, February 1986, and previous issues.

[a]Billions of dollars.

[b]Includes public assistance, Medicaid, SSI and food stamps.

[c]Includes vocational rehabilitation, institutional care, child welfare and nutrition, state and local anti-poverty and manpower programs and legal assistance.

order of 3.5 percent. At the same time, however, real (inflation-adjusted) disposable income rose 6.2 percent over the same four years. Assuming an income elasticity of .75, we would expect a rise in money donations of 4.6 percent. Thus, the net result of price and income effects would have been to increase contribu-

Table 9.3
Revenue Sources of Social Service Nonprofit Organizations, Various Years, 1977–1984[a]

Year	Private Donations	Payments Private	Payments Government	Investment Income	Total Revenue
1977	3.6	1.1	6.1	0.3	11.4
1980	3.7	1.4	6.2	0.4	12.0
1982	4.0	1.4	5.6	0.3	11.6
1983	4.4	1.5	5.6	0.4	12.2
1984	4.7	1.6	5.5	0.4	12.5
% Change 1977-84	30.6	45.5	-9.8	33.3	9.6
% Change 1980-84	27.0	14.0	-11.3	0.0	4.2

Source: Hodgkinson and Weitzman, 1986, p. 117.

[a]In billions of inflation-adjusted (1977) dollars.

tions by approximately 1.1 percent over four years. However, real giving to social welfare rose by much more than this—27 percent. Thus, it appears that donors did respond to government cutbacks by increasing their giving.[13]

While giving did respond, it only approximately compensated for the direct loss in government revenue experienced by charities. Again, a simple calculation is useful. If we net out the estimated 1.1 percent increase in giving brought about by income and price changes, the "unexplained" portion of the increase amounts to $750 million.[14] Even if this is entirely due to changes in government spending, it is not much more than the $700 million loss in government revenues. Thus, while increased giving allowed the charitable sector to maintain its current level of revenue, it was not sufficient to allow a significant expansion.

Charities Turn to Sales

The cutback in government support also encouraged charities to increase their use of fees as well as their commercial sales (Table 9.3). Private payments (other than donations) rose, in real terms, by $200 million, or 14 percent, over the four years. As noted, the recent tax reform is likely to accelerate this move toward commerciality.

WHAT DOES THE FUTURE HOLD?

Predicting the future for the charitable sector is extremely hazardous. Not only is it necessary to predict the responses of donors and charities to changes in policy—a difficult undertaking in and of itself—but one must also attempt to guess what those policy changes will be.[15]

On the tax side, it is unlikely that there will be large changes for the charitable sector in the near future. Congress appears reluctant to consider major changes in the tax code for at least the next several years, preferring to let taxpayers adjust to the 1986 changes. In addition, the continuing federal budget deficits make it unlikely that new subsidies to giving, such as the restoration of the "above-the-line" deduction, will be introduced into the tax code.

If there are no major changes in the tax code, it seems likely that the average of giving will fall slightly, as real income growth and inflation make it worthwhile for a larger proportion of taxpayers to itemize. If budget deficits force the next administration to raise income tax rates, particularly for the wealthy, prices may fall substantially.

On the spending side, it again appears as though there will be little in the way of new initiatives. Pressure will remain to reduce the budget deficit, at least in part, via domestic spending cuts. Thus charities should not expect government support to increase dramatically. At the same time, however, further cutbacks will continue to increase the need for charitable services. Thus, the search for new, particularly commercial, sources of support is likely to accelerate. Even here, however, charities are likely to face roadblocks. The next few years will probably see legislative efforts to make it more difficult for nonprofit organizations to compete with for-profit firms in commercial activities. The creativity and perseverance of the charitable sector will be sorely tested in the years ahead.

NOTES

1. This represents a consensus estimate in the literature, although my estimate is considerable higher (see Chapter 6).

2. This rise in itemization was brought about largely by inflation, which reduced the real value of the standard deduction.

3. In 1982, non-itemizers were allowed a deduction for only 25 percent of the first $100 of donations. By 1985, 50 percent of all charitable gifts were deductible by non-itemizers.

4. The impact of changes in the distribution of income is also typically taken into account.

5. This is true for volunteering to some sorts of charity and for some volunteer activities.

6. For details, see Schiff (1987).

7. Hodgkinson and Weitzman (1986), p. 11.

8. *New York Times*, February 15, 1985, p. 1, "Corporate Giving Fails to Offset Cuts by U.S."

9. *New York Times*, March 10, 1987, p. 48, "For Nonprofit Theatres, A Victory Over Red Ink."

10. These are payments from government to private nonprofit organizations to finance the provision of social services.

11. Note, however, that if a charity's manager wishes to maximize the quantity of services provided, he or she will have an incentive to ensure efficient provision.

12. They will likely also be forced to make do with less government support. I discuss this below.

13. In Chapter 8, I argued that there was no "Reagan effect." This does not imply that donors failed to respond to changes in government spending; rather, it means that their response was no greater than our model would have predicted.

14. Again this is expressed as real, 1977 dollars.

15. Of course, other factors, such as demographic changes, will influence the future of the charitable sector.

Bibliography

Abrams, Burton, and Mark Schmitz. "The Crowding-Out Effect of Government Transfers on Private Charitable Contributions," *Public Choice*, 33, 1978, 29–37.

———. "The Crowding-Out Effect of Government Transfers on Private Charitable Contributions: Cross-Section Evidence," *National Tax Journal*, 37, December 1984, 563–68.

Akerlof, George. "The Market for Lemons: Quality Uncertainty and the Market Mechanism," *Quarterly Journal of Economics*, 84, August 1970, 485–500.

Auten, Gerald, and Gabriel Rudney. "The Variability of Charitable Giving," unpublished paper, February 1988.

Boskin, Michael, and Martin Feldstein. "Effects of the Charitable Deduction on Contributions by Low Income and Middle Income Households: Evidence from the National Survey of Philanthropy," *Review of Economics and Statistics*, 59, August 1977, 351–54.

Buchanan, James. "Ethical Rules, Expected Values and Large Numbers," *Ethics*, 76, October 1965, 1–13.

Clotfelter, Charles. "Tax Incentives and Charitable Giving: Evidence from a Panel of Taxpayers," *Journal of Public Economics*, 13, June 1980, 319–40.

———. *Federal Tax Policy and Charitable Giving*. Chicago: University of Chicago Press, 1985.

————. "Life After Tax Reform for Higher Education," unpublished paper, Duke University, 1987.

Dye, Richard. "Contributions of Volunteer Time: Some Evidence of Income Tax Effects," *National Tax Journal*, 33, March 1980, 89–93.

Feldstein, Martin. "The Income Tax and Charitable Contributions: Part 1—Aggregate and Distributional Effects," *National Tax Journal*, 28, March 1975, 81–100.

————. "The Income Tax and Charitable Contributions: Part 2—The Impact on Religious, Educational and Other Organizations," *National Tax Journal*, 28, June 1975, 209–25.

Feldstein, Martin, and Charles Clotfelter. "Tax Incentives and Charitable Contributions in the U.S.: A Microeconometric Analysis," *Journal of Public Economics*, 5, January 1976, 1–26.

Feldstein, Martin, and Amy Taylor. "The Income Tax and Charitable Contributions," *Econometrica*, 44, November 1976, 1201–22.

The Gallup Organization. *Americans Volunteer 1985*. Washington, D.C.: Independent Sector, 1986.

Hansmann, Henry. "The Role of Nonprofit Enterprise," *Yale Law Journal*, 89, April 1980, 835–901.

Hartogs, Nelly. *Impact of Government Funding on the Management of Voluntary Agencies*. New York: The Greater New York United Way, 1978.

Hey, John. *Uncertainty in Microeconomics*. New York: New York University Press, 1979.

Hirschman, Albert. *Exit, Voice and Loyalty*. Cambridge, Mass.: Harvard University Press, 1970.

Hochman, Harold, and James Rodgers. "The Optimal Treatment of Charitable Contributions," *National Tax Journal*, 30, March 1977, 1–18.

Hodgkinson, Virginia, and Murray Weitzman. *Dimensions of the Independent Sector: A Statistical Profile*. Washington, D.C.: Independent Sector, 1986.

Kihlstrom, Richard. "A Bayesian Model of Demand for Information About Product Quality," *International Economic Review*, 15, February 1974, 99–118.

Lindsey, Lawrence. "Individual Giving Under the Tax Reform Act of 1986," *The Constitution and the Independent Sector: 1987 Spring Research Forum Working Papers*. Washington, D.C.: Independent Sector, 1987, 133–46.

Lindsey, Lawrence, and Richard Steinberg. "Joint Crowdout: An Empirical Study of the Effects of Federal Grants on State Government Expenditures and Local Donations," unpublished paper, February 1988.

Long, Stephen. "Income Tax Effects on Donor Choice of Money and Time Contributions," *National Tax Journal*, 30, June 1977, 207–12.

Mackay, Robert, and Gerald Whitney. "The Comparative Statics of Quantity Constraints and Conditional Demands: Theory and Applications," *Econometrica*, 48, November 1980, 1727–43.

Menchik, Paul, and Burton Weisbrod. "Voluntary Factor Provision in the Supply of Collective Goods," in Michelle White, ed., *Nonprofit Firms in a Three Sector Economy*. Washington, D.C.: Urban Institute, 1981.

———. "Volunteer Labor Supply," *Journal of Public Economics*, 32 (2), March 1987, 159–84.

Mueller, Marnie. "Economic Determinants of Volunteer Work by Women," *Signs*, Winter 1975, 325–38.

Niskanen, William. "Bureaucrats and Politicians," *Journal of Law and Economics*, 18, December 1975, 617–43.

Olson, Mancur. *The Logic of Collective Action*. New York: Schocken Books, 1965.

Pollack, Robert. "Conditional Demand Functions and Consumption Theory," *Quarterly Journal of Economics*, 83, February 1969, 60–78.

Reece, William. "Charitable Contributions: New Evidence on Household Behavior," *American Economic Review*, 69, March 1979, 142–51.

Reece, William, and Kimberly Zieschang. "Consistent Estimation of the Impact of Tax Deductibility on the Level of Charitable Contributions," *Econometrica*, 53, March 1985, 271–93.

Roberts, Russell. "A Positive Model of Private Charity and Public Transfers," *Journal of Political Economy*, 92, February 1984, 136–48.

Rose-Ackerman, Susan. "United Charities: An Economic Analysis," *Public Policy*, 28, Summer 1980, 323–50.

———. "Do Government Grants to Charity Reduce Private Donations?" in Michelle White, ed. *Nonprofit Firms in a Three Sector Economy*. Washington, D.C.: Urban Institute, 1981.

———. "Do Government Grants to Charity Reduce Private Donations?" in Susan Rose-Ackerman, ed., *The Economics of Nonprofit Institutions: Studies in Structure and Policy*. New York: Oxford University Press, 1986, 313–31.

————. "Ideals versus Dollars: Donors, Charity Managers, and Government Grants," *Journal of Political Economy*, 95, August 1987.

Rosen, Sherwin. "Learning and Experience in the Labor Market," *Journal of Human Resources*, 7, Summer 1972, 326–42.

Salamon, Lester, and Alan Abramson. "Nonprofits and the Federal Budget: Deeper Cuts Ahead," *Foundation News*, March/April 1985, 48–54.

Schiff, Jerald. "Does Government Spending Crowd Out Charitable Giving?" *National Tax Journal*, 38, December 1985, 535–46.

————. "Tax Reform and Volunteering," *The Constitution and the Independent Sector: 1987 Spring Research Forum Working Papers*. Washington, D.C.: Indendent Sector, 1987, 147–57.

————. "Tax Policy, Charitable Giving and the Nonprofit Sector: What Do We Really Know?" in Richard Magat, ed. *Philanthropic Giving*. New York: Oxford University Press, 1989.

Schiff, Jerald, and Burton Weisbrod. "Government Social Welfare Spending and the Private Nonprofit Sector: Crowding-Out, and More," unpublished paper, November 1986.

————. "Competition Between Nonprofit and For-Profit Firms in Commercial Markets," unpublished paper, 1987.

Schwartz, Robert. "Personal Philanthropic Contributions," *Journal of Political Economy*, 78, November 1970, 1264–91.

Smith, Bruce L.R., and Nelson Rosenbaum. "The Fiscal Capacity of the Nonprofit Sector," Brookings Institution, December 1981.

Steinberg, Richard. "Should Donors Care About Fundraising?" in Susan Rose-Ackerman, ed. *The Economics of Nonprofit Institutions: Studies in Structure and Policy*. New York: Oxford University Press, 1986, 347–65.

————. "The Revealed Objective of Nonprofit Firms," *Rand Journal of Economics*, 17 (4), Winter 1986, 508–26.

————. "Voluntary Donations and Public Expenditures in a Federalist System," *American Economic Review*, 77 (1), March 1987, 24–36.

Survey Research Center. *The National Survey of Philanthropy*. Ann Arbor: University of Michigan, 1974.

Taussig, Michael. "Economic Aspects of the Personal Income Tax Treatment of Charitable Contributions," *National Tax Journal*, 20, March 1967, 1–19.

Tiebout, Charles. "A Pure Theory of Public Expenditures," *Journal of Political Economy*, 64, October 1956, 416–24.

Tobin, James. "Estimation of Relationships for Limited Dependent Variables," *Econometrica*, 26, January 1958, 24–36.

Warr, Peter. "Pareto Optimal Redistribution and Private Charity," *Journal of Public Economics*, 18, October 1982, 131–138.

Weisbrod, Burton. "Toward a Theory of the Voluntary Nonprofit Sector in a Three Sector Economy," in Edmund Phelps, ed. *Altruism, Morality and Economic Theory*. New York: Russell Sage Foundation, 1975.

Weisbrod, Burton, and Nestor Dominguez. "Demand for Collective Goods in Private Nonprofit Markets: Can Fundraising Expenditures Help Overcome Free Rider Behavior?" *Journal of Public Economics*, 30, June 1986, 83–96.

Yankelovich, Skelly and White Inc. *The Charitable Behavior of Americans*. Washington, D.C.: Independent Sector, 1986.

Index

About the Author

JERALD SCHIFF, formerly Assistant Professor of Economics at
Tulane University, is an economist at the International Monetary
Fund. Previously he worked for the Treasuries of the United States
and New Zealand. He has contributed articles to *National Tax
Journal, Philanthropic Monthly,* and *Contemporary Issues in Fund
Raising,* and has written a chapter in *Philanthropic Giving* (forth-
coming).